You Are Your Own Best Teacher!
Sparking the Curiosity, Imagination, and Intellect of Tweens

"In this unique volume, Claire Nader speaks to the next generation, the leaders who will be. In Indigenous thinking there is a clear mandate to raise leaders, and not coddle the next generation, understanding that we must consider the impact of our decisions on the seven generations ahead—intergenerational responsibility. In times of chaos, Nader illuminates the power of youth, and their creative minds to challenge practices that most adults have accepted as a pre-ordained reality. She reminds her readers that the strongest skill in the face of these times lies with our youth change makers; and their access to imagination and creativity. Great changes are made when these innate gifts are combined with critical thinking and courage. Miigwech."
—WINONA LADUKE, Executive Director, Honor the Earth

"Claire Nader has issued a clarion call to our society's youth to harness their imagination and follow their own path forward. *You Are Your Own Best Teacher!* is a bold, inspiring invitation to children to embrace inner strengths and forge the positive future the world so desperately needs."
—AMY GOODMAN, *Democracy Now!*

"If you are a tween or a family member seeking empowering ideas and inspiration in these tough times, Claire Nader's book is for you. She reminds us of the power of tweens—those who develop questioning minds, character, courage and idealism—to change our world. Think Greta!"
—KATRINA VANDEN HEUVAL, Editorial Director and Publisher, *The Nation*

"Claire Nader's book will surprise and excite 'tweens' about the power they have to make a difference in our corporate-dominated world. But adult readers will also be awakened and empowered by this beautifully crafted book. Her wisdom brings a smile to your face and essential insight for these grim times. *You Are Your Own Best Teacher!* is truly a book for all ages."
—CHARLES DERBER, Professor of Sociology at Boston College and author of *Corporation Nation and Welcome to the Revolution.*

"Claire Nader's, *You Are Your Own Best Teacher!*, is a sage, inspiring, and illuminating book. Written in a conversational style and directed to tweens, the book is an especially valuable tool for parents and teachers who want to help children make smart choices that will equip them to lead satisfying, meaningful lives while growing up and as adult members of their communities."
—NANCY NEWMAN, author, *Raising Passionate Readers*

"The book highlights the importance of self-education on how to achieve 'a life well-lived' to arguably the most important generation of our times. The narrative style of the work has many sections, each of which provides important lessons. The book is exciting to read and I will recommend it to my ten-year-old grandson to stimulate his own critical thinking and self-education through concentration, imagination, curiosity, and empathy."
—NICHOLAS A. ASHFORD, Professor of Technology and Policy, Massachusetts Institute of Technology

"Claire Nader has written an inspirational book for young people that empowers this special age group to call on their creativity and moral sensibility to see—and change—the world around them. It is a welcome, loving antidote to the corporate and social-media forces that 'sell' young people as a product."
—JANE HALL, Associate Professor, School of Communication, American University, Washington, DC

"Tweens like to be included in the conversation, spoken to like adults. Nader does not talk down to them. She speaks to them as equals and reminds them of all the great things they can do now and in the future. She inspires them with amazing deeds that have been performed by kids their own age and goes on to open doors for them to be great themselves. This is not just a 'How to' book, it leads by example of others who have gone before and covers lots of territory: health, personal hygiene, history—ancestors, becoming an ancestor yourself, laws, justice, nature, animals, to mention a few. I was inspired to look up the famous quote from Margaret Mead which I will now misquote: 'Never doubt that a small group of thoughtful, committed kids can change the world; it's among the only things that ever have.'"
—HELENE Z. HILL, PH.D. Professor Emerita,
Radiation Biology, Rutgers University and Author

"This work by Claire Nader is extraordinary. She comments on a myriad of issues in a way that children can understand. More importantly, she illuminates the misleading practices of adults and renders sage advice. She integrates contemporary and historical examples to make her points come alive. All in all, this book is full of wisdom—more than any other I have read in my 76 years on this earth. And it is written with subtle humor and the clever use of examples. I wish I could have read it to my two sons. None of us would fall asleep and all of us would grow wiser.
—PROF. ROBERT C. FELLMETH, Price Professor of
Public Interest Law, University of San Diego Law School,
Executive Director of the Children's Advocacy Institute

"An important book that will stimulate today's social media-saturated kids to put down their phones and realize that they can change the world now by harnessing their natural curiosity and imagination, and opening their minds to knowledge that cannot be learned in the classroom."
—RICHARD PANCHYK, author of 47 books, many for children.

*Sofie:
I read this book and found it to be informative even for a 91 year old
Love
Mortar aka Tartar
December 2024*

You Are Your Own Best Teacher!

TWEENS—A BOOK FOR YOU AND YOUR FAMILY

You Are Your Own Best Teacher!

Sparking the Curiosity, Imagination, and Intellect of Tweens

Claire Nader

Essential Books
Washington, DC

Copyright © 2022 by Claire Nader

All rights reserved. No part of this publication may be reproduced, distributed, or transmitted in any form or by any means, including photocopying, recording, or other electronic or mechanical methods, without the prior written permission of the publisher, except in the case of brief quotations embodied in reviews and certain other noncommercial uses permitted by copyright law. For permission requests, write to the publisher at the address below.

Attention: Permissions Coordinator
Essential Books
P.O. Box 19405
Washington, DC 20036

Library of Congress Control Number: 2022934983

ISBN: 978-1-893520-00-4 (hardcover)
ISBN: 978-1-893520-04-2 (paperback)

Printed in the USA.

First Edition 2022

9 8 7 6 5 4 3 2 1

To my parents and siblings who created a climate for spirited dialogue about the common good as we were growing up, and to the youngsters in their pre-teen years who along with their parents engaged my impromptu repartees over time.

CONTENTS

ACKNOWLEDGMENT xiii

A Beautiful Spark 1
The Truth About Kids 7
The Truth About School 12
Let's Talk About Screens 16
Time Out for Gratitude 18
Playing Different Roles Expands the Mind 19
Concentration, Imagination, and Curiosity 22
What If? 23
Social Action: An Urge to Improve the World 24
Fifth-Grade Firebrands 27
Peer Groups and Other Outside Pressures 30
Order in the Classroom Versus Critical Thinking 33
Company Ads and Deceptions 36
The Dark Side 40
Maturity at an Early Age 43
The Dictionary: A Door to Meaning, Understanding,
    and Enchantment 49
Being Smart 57
Solitude 61
History Infused with Myths 63
Unlearning to Learn 67
Learning by Doing 69
Self-Education Can Be the Best Medicine 71
Addictions 74
Who's Raising You Anyway? 76
Talking Back: Controlling What We
    the People Already Own! 79
Young Inventors and Tween Talk Shows 80
The Importance of a Questioning Mind 84

Family Stories	87
Family Discussions	90
Beyond Family Discussions	93
Discovering How You're Controlled by Companies	96
Good Companies	100
Three Historic Americans: Beating the Odds Through Self-Education	102
Frames of Reference Revisited	127
Moving from Knowledge to Action: Developing Healthy Habits	133
Becoming an Informed Consumer	139
Your Own Body	144
Becoming a Good Ancestor	150
Becoming a Smart Voter	152
Becoming Alert to Propaganda	153
What Happened to Physical Education in Schools?	161
The Beauty Business	163
The Two Great Pillars of Our Civil Justice System	167
Taboos and the Classroom	183
Smoking: A Case Study in Confronting Power	185
Citizen Action/Community Action: What Is It?	189
The Discipline of Discovery	195
A Side Note on Proverbs	199
Holidays: What We Celebrate	202
"War Is a Racket"	204
Waging Peace, Not War	207
Colman McCarthy and Peace Studies	208
Animal Welfare and Respecting Nature	214
A Fond Farewell	221
INDEX	225
ABOUT THE AUTHOR	237

ACKNOWLEDGMENT

Heartfelt thanks to Joy Johannessen, a wise editor, Jean Bauer who patiently typed the manuscript, and John Richard of Essential Books who took us to the finish line with his customary care. My gratitude to Ralph Nader who recognized my penchant for conversing with youngsters as the inspiration for this book.

You Are Your Own Best Teacher!

A Beautiful Spark

If you are between the ages of nine and twelve—that is, if you're a tween—this book is for you. If you're a little younger or a little older, don't worry, you'll find much of value in these pages as well, as long as you're someone who wants to take greater charge of your own education and your own role in the world around you.

What's so special, you may ask me, about the years between nine and twelve? In my experience, these are the years when you're at the peak of inspiration, idealism, and frank questioning. In my conversations over the years with kids in your age group, I'm always amazed at their imagination and their undiluted idealism about what the world should be like but is not. At nine or ten, you begin wondering why the world is so full of violence, pollution, racism, hunger, poverty, and disease, and why adults aren't doing something about these conditions, especially those which have known solutions. As you enter your teenage years, other concerns, desires, and diversions may start crowding out these priceless traits of imagination and idealism—unless you become more self-aware before you become a teenager.

We adults need to encourage more of your pure imaginative idealism and your practical demands to fix problems. Your idealism is a beautiful spark that should fire us all up rather than be dismissed, as it too often is, as a flight of childhood. Marianne Carus, who founded the well-received magazine *Cricket* in 1973, did not condescend to youngsters, instead providing them with regular serious fun for their expanding and imaginative minds. In 1982, she told the *Baltimore Sun*, "So many people talk down to children, but you have to respect their intelligence. Parents give them the best clothes, the best food, the best toys, when what they should be giving them is food for their little brains."

Unlike *Cricket* and its founder, many adults may tell you that you're too young to understand complex issues, too young to be engaged in social activism, too young to make your voices heard. They may tell you that you have to wait until you're older.

Greta Thunberg didn't wait. She was nine when she began studying climate disruptions and the increasing damage they inflicted on communities all over the world. She collected the essential facts about the magnitude and frequency of these climate devastations—wildfires, droughts, floods, hurricanes, ice melts in the Arctic and Antarctic—and through cogent science-based arguments, she enlisted her parents and her sister to endorse her personal philosophy: to step lightly on this earth, our only home. In 2018, when she was fifteen, she began her Friday school strikes in front of the Swedish parliament building to call for action on climate change, and the next year, addressing the United Nations, she demanded bluntly, "How dare you steal our future through inaction?" Her challenge resonated throughout the world.

Felix Finkbeiner didn't wait. In 2007, when he was nine, he was enthralled by Wangari Maathai, a Kenyan woman whose life work was to restore the forests of her country, earning her a Nobel Peace Prize in 2004. She founded the Green Belt Movement in 1977, enlisting poor women to plant tens of millions of trees at a cost of a few shillings per tree. Felix decided that he was going to make something similar happen in Germany and around the world, but his goal was a billion trees. One billion trees! He knew that the more trees we have, the fewer greenhouse gases are emitted to disrupt the planet's climate. He got to work, learning along the way. As he labored, Felix caught the attention of enough people in groups worldwide to meet his ambitious goal before he turned eighteen. His messages and mailings and journeys were just that motivating for people who were astonished by the maturity and determination of this very informed, resilient boy from Germany. And his very young age generated a kind of powerful communication in and of itself, because his call for action is not what adults expect from kids.

Autumn Pelletier didn't wait. She comes from a culture that does not rest on conquering nature but on blending with it. She is Anishinaabe from Wikwemikong First Nation Unceded Territory on Manitoulin Island within Lake Huron, in Ontario, Canada. In the Anishinaabe world view, water and all living things are sacred. At age eight, Autumn learned that her community's drinking water was contaminated, and that peril turned her into a "Water Warrior." In 2016, at age twelve, she publicly confronted Prime Minister Justin Trudeau at a First Nations Assembly and scolded him for failing to protect the water. At thirteen, she spoke at Waterworld Day at the United Nations General Assembly, advocating for clean drinking water for coming generations. Autumn reminds us that "Mother Earth has been in existence for billions of years. She doesn't need us, but we need her."

Cavanaugh Bell was only seven years old when he began working to improve the lives of the people in his town of Gaithersburg, Maryland, and as far away as the Pine Ridge Indian Reservation in South Dakota. A second grader, he reacted to being bullied by using his own savings to put together care packages of groceries and supplies for the elderly in town. Social media took notice, and soon donations enabled Cavanaugh and his mother, Llacey Simmons, to open a food pantry in a nearby donated warehouse space. Consider the way he described himself on his GoFundMe page, as reported in a long feature in the *Washington Post* in late 2020: "After I was bullied and I felt a darkness inside of me, I knew I didn't want other kids to feel the same way I felt. So, I asked my mom if she could help me spread love and positivity. And, the more I gave back to my community, the more I wanted to keep doing it."

Cavanaugh responded to adversity (in preschool he stopped eating for a time because of the bullying) by expanding his charitable giving, fueled by admiring adults who couldn't believe this little boy's self-motivation. Traveling with his mother through the Pine Ridge Reservation en route to Mount Rushmore, he was stunned by its stark poverty. Back home, he turned to social media to ask for donations, which poured in to fill two semi-trucks with food, blankets, jackets, and other essential items needed by the thousands of families there. The more Cavanaugh did, the more news coverage he received and the more ideas he came up with for people to help. "Cavanaugh just blew my mind. The way he speaks from his soul and his heart," said Kathleen Blair, a resident of Churchill Senior Living in Germantown, Maryland. She had seen all the care packages Cavanaugh and his mom had been dropping off at Churchill for months, and soon she and the other residents began assembling care packages for Pine Ridge.

While encouraging the cycle of giving, helped along by more and more volunteers, Cavanaugh continued to speak out against bullying, not forgetting what had led him to open up so many windows of positivity for so many people. Now about nine years old, and as observant as ever, he keeps devising specific assistance projects that spark helpful responses almost effortlessly, telling the *Post*, "I want people to know that they can do anything—it doesn't matter if you are eight or eighty-seven, you can make change. You just need to believe it."

That's Cavanaugh—all of eight and going on twenty-five!

On April 24, 2021, the *New York Times* ran an article by Anne Barnard with the eye-grabbing headline "N.Y.C. Bans Pesticides in Parks with Push from Unlikely Force: Children." Barnard traced this marvelous result back to forces set in motion by Paula Rogovin and her kindergarten class at a Manhattan public school in 2014. Over the next seven years, as her students entered their early teens, they were joined by their parents and by activist groups that put constant pressure on city officials, which led to the passage of the pesticide ban by the New York City Council on Earth Day 2021. Council member Ben Kallos recalled that he had been persuaded by "a bunch of kindergartners" to propose a ban on pesticides on city-owned land back in 2014 but had met with resistance from City Hall and the Parks Department, even after he held "the best, cutest hearing ever" in 2017, during which the council chamber was filled with children singing "This Land Is Your Land."

Paula Rogovin retired in 2018 after forty-four years of teaching, but she stayed with the mission as her original kindergartners grew up and held rallies and generated human energy that culminated in the ban. Their passionate effort educated a force of intergenerational activists, and it all began when their teacher explained that turtles like their class pet, Soccer Ball, could be poisoned, a prospect that horrified her students. "Ban toxic pesticides! Use only Nature's pesticides! Pass. A. Law!" was their chant and their goal. They built a movement "toward natural management that's good for our health, the environment and the planet," said Jay Feldman, the energetic executive director of Beyond Pesticides, a national advocacy group that supported the citywide ban.

If you're surprised by what youngsters like you can do, maybe it's because you're not self-conscious enough to recognize what observing adults have noticed forever. At your age, you are free to ask questions and to call for ready solutions to conditions going in the wrong direction. You can see the solutions separately from the entanglements of the grown-up world where a few powerful people control the organizations that keep solutions from helping everyone else. This freedom of yours explains your inclination to raise the essential "why" questions about climate disruptions, pollution, social injustice, and a host of other problems. As one middle schooler asked, "If pollution is so dangerous to our health, why isn't it illegal?" I noticed the same practical approach many years ago when children pressed their parents to quit smoking or wear seatbelts once they learned that such smart moves saved lives.

It is because you ask why obvious improvements to bad conditions aren't applied that you are very important to making grown-ups create a better world. Adults find their better selves come forth in response to children asking why bad conditions have to be the way they are and why they can't be changed for the common good.

There are many more examples of remarkable young people like Greta, Felix, Autumn, Cavanaugh, and Paula Rogovin's class—fifth graders in Salt Lake City who exposed a toxic waste dump near their school, fifth graders in Chicago who launched a campaign to fix their decrepit school, a boy of ten who saw people in Africa walking tremendous distances and asked, "Why not give them bicycles?" I'll tell you more about them later on. For now I'll just say that this book is a labor of love, meant to show you how much of your potential can be fulfilled through your own self-reliant, imaginative thinking, envisioning, and doing. You may be amazed beyond your greatest expectations.

The Truth About Kids

My brother Ralph likes to tell a secret about politicians, especially when they're running for office. They are wary of being asked questions by youngsters like you than by anyone else, even seasoned reporters. He's often suggested sending the White House press corps on a week's vacation and replacing them with tweens, then watching as the president's press secretary squirms in the face of a torrent of dart-like questions that don't hedge or come with sandpapered self-censorship. You see, you're at an age of full candor unless you're ordered otherwise. You don't speak with what poets have called "forked tongues," you don't get mired down in trying to avoid saying what you really want to say. You are not burdened by all those invisible chains placed on reporters by their cowardly media bosses.

The great groundbreaking journalist Helen Thomas drove presidents and press secretaries up the wall during her sixty-year career as a White House correspondent and author. Why? Because she repeatedly asked questions like the ones you'd ask—direct questions such as "Mr. President, why are we in Iraq?" or "What about the rights of Palestinians under Israeli occupation?"—and repeatedly received evasive replies. Fox News reporter Brit Hume used to fume at Helen when he wasn't playing tennis with George W. Bush. He thought it was unprofessional of her to interject her opinions through her questions. How naive can a self-censoring reporter be? Long before Brit Hume fumed at Helen Thomas, long before he became a rich man and a bullhorn for the Bushes, he was a young investigative reporter exposing the horrible crimes of the coal industry and other corporate abuses while working for the brave, dynamic, widely syndicated columnist Jack Anderson, who had opinions that drove his news sense.

Once, on the campaign trail, a young girl somehow managed to ask President Ronald Reagan a question: "Where does most of our pollution come from?" Few reporters would ever ask such a directly factual question. Mr. Reagan blinked and replied, "Why, eighty percent of pollution comes from trees." The reporters covering the event groaned and moved to correct Mr. Reagan's arboreal waywardness. The youngster had unwittingly unmasked his environmental ignorance in a way that a hundred reporters couldn't or wouldn't do.

On May 14, 2017, the *New York Times* published a special kids' section. On the back page was a simple list that you may find enjoyable and intriguing. Here it is.

The truth is kids want to be part of the conversation.
The truth is kids are more curious than many adults.
The truth is kids know that lies are bad.
The truth is kids think cash is still cool.
The truth is kids don't let differences divide them.
The truth is kids learn something new every day.
The truth is kids are smarter than you think.
The truth is kids can turn any place into a playground.
The truth is kids can make a difference right now.
The truth is kids feel things as deeply as adults do.
The truth is kids don't need candy to feel better.
The truth is kids will inherit the earth.
The truth is kids have big dreams.
The truth is kids want to discover the world.

> The truth is kids expect honesty.
> The truth is kids think the simple stuff is funny.
> The truth is kids bring people together.
> The truth is kids appreciate a good story.
> The truth is kids can handle the truth.

Well, well, well! By now you may be feeling pretty good about yourself. Do you agree with some or most or all of these statements? Ponder them. Maybe you'll want to add a few of your own, for example:

The truth is kids want to be good ancestors.

Robert Clampitt, a retired Wall Street lawyer, did his best to be a good ancestor. In 1975, with his own money, he founded Children's Express to give kids between ten and thirteen an opportunity to be reporters, to write articles, conduct interviews, and provide commentary on current affairs in a pioneering new youth magazine. He believed that their curiosity and lack of inhibition were perfect qualifications for a career in journalism. A short time later, during the 1976 Democratic National Convention, a Children's Express reporter, thirteen-year-old Gilbert Giles, scooped the adult reporters by revealing that Walter Mondale would be Jimmy Carter's pick for vice-president.

Over the next twenty years, CE reporters in their distinctive yellow shirts expanded from their original office in New York to bureaus in several other states, England, and Japan. Their articles, edited by teenagers and adults, covered a large variety of topics from the youth viewpoint. They dug into stories about school violence, civil rights, abortion, politics, the environment, consumer protection, and legislation affecting youngsters. They started a newswire so that papers and magazines across the country could pick up their stories. The CE news magazine sometimes made national television, including PBS prime time. They won major journalism awards for their coverage of the 1988 presidential campaign. CE reporters from the bureau in Washington, DC, were admitted to White House press briefings and continued to cover presidential elections.

In 1996, founder and chief fundraiser Robert Clampitt died suddenly, and the organization ran out of money in 2000, when it closed. Nevertheless, for twenty-five years, Children's Express proved the maturity of youngsters under the pressure of getting the news accurately and on deadline in a field hitherto reserved for trained adults. Moreover, they were able to ask politicians and public figures short, direct, cutting questions, unlike many adult journalists. I remember watching a show hosted by NBC's famous anchorman David Brinkley, who had invited a trio of CE reporters to interview Vice-President Nelson Rockefeller during the Republican National Convention in 1976. One of them, a ten-year-old, asked Rockefeller, "Why are you still supporting President Gerald Ford after he just dumped you in favor of another candidate?" After Mr. Rockefeller made the expected polite response to conclude the interview, David Brinkley declared with a smile, "I wish we could ask questions like that!"

Astonishingly, despite CE's great success and expansion, there were not enough good ancestors to pick up where Robert Clampitt left off and provide the modest financial support needed to continue. Today there are a variety of programs meant to encourage young people to become reporters, including National Public Radio's internship programs for junior journalists and the American Society of News Editors Youth Journalism Initiative, but they cannot compare with Children's Express and the responsibility it gave its young, self-reliant reporters to operate an independent news service.

If children had their own serious, exciting news program on our public airwaves, as they should have had when the television age started, there would have been nourishing roots for a Children's Express all over the country. Unfortunately, the elders in Congress and in the White House were not up to the challenge decades ago when they gave away the people's airwaves free to commercial radio and television stations that produced cartoons and violent movies targeted at children and endlessly stacked with advertisements for junk food, soda, military toys, and other harmful products. I have found that using the words "good ancestors" in your questions to adults gets them thinking about what they're handing down to your generation so you can be proud of them. Or not.

The Truth About School

I was your age once. It was a time of rapid learning. I learned in school, at home, at our local Beardsley and Memorial Library, and I taught myself a few things. Guess what I remember most: what I learned at home from my parents and what I taught myself. As I moved into early adulthood, I found myself wishing that more of my learning had come from home and from me.

Schools and teachers are experiencing rough times, and that was so even before the Covid-19 pandemic of 2020 forced schools to close and teachers to conduct their classes online. Teachers are swamped by constant required multiple-choice testing to measure you against other students. They are often short of all kinds of classroom materials, and often pay for what they need out of their own pockets. If they undertake anything controversial—such as helping you to *think* critically instead of telling you what to *believe*—people and groups outside the school jump on them. Such pressure to avoid robust questioning keeps teachers from applying techniques they know to engage you in exciting explorations of the world and people around you, from your own community on up to the national and international levels of human activity.

When it comes to your schooling, the best teachers realize there is much you need to know that is not taught in classrooms or found on your computer screens. They also know that the more you pick up from their teaching and continue on your own, the deeper your education will be. To quote Mark Twain, author of *The Adventures of Huckleberry Finn* and a lifelong practitioner of self-learning, "I have never let my schooling interfere with my education."

As you grow older, you'll realize increasingly what you did *not* learn and what you need to *unlearn*. You'll realize that there are many things you could have absorbed more easily at your age than later in your life, especially foreign languages. Knowledge, not just facts, that is very personal to your well-being and your "pursuit of happiness," in the immortal words of Thomas Jefferson, is what this little book is all about. It aims to give you a head start on your teenage years so that you're equipped to navigate them prudently and with a steady hand.

I am mindful of how different from one another young readers are likely to be. You are different in what interests you, where you live, how you think, what and whom you know, and other conditions such as your family situation, income, health, and safety. You are different in your worries and hopes, and in what space and time you have for self-learning. I am mindful too that I often write from a perspective that assumes your family is relatively well off, living in a safe neighborhood with access to good schools and good nutrition, but I know that we live in a nation of brutal poverty where control of the wealth is in the hands of 1 percent of the population. If you don't live in a safe and prosperous neighborhood, you may be asking your parents why you can't have what your better-off peers have, a form of psychological damage along with material deprivation.

If you're among the privileged and you live in a neighborhood free of the scourges of poverty and violence, a neighborhood of tree-lined streets, clean air and water, no daily sirens, and no hunger at all, you might want to start imagining such a better world, that you can see on the internet from time to time. You might want to start asking adults questions that go right to the heart of your fears and your beautiful compassion for your less fortunate peers.

Throughout this book, I seek to recognize the diversity of my readers and at the same time to find as much common ground about your needs, joys, and excitement as possible while offering you self-education suggestions from which you can choose. As you read, I hope you will welcome my belief in your capacity and willingness to understand beyond what many grown-ups think your age group can absorb. Our society often underestimates you, categorizes or labels you too rigidly. It doesn't allow you to discover just how good, smart, and idealistic you truly can be *right now*, especially if you are given a chance.

As you've seen from Greta Thunberg and the other young activists I've mentioned, regular youngsters like you have produced amazing achievements. How? They just found ways to open their own doors and windows and teach themselves to bring off these jaw-dropping accomplishments. Sometimes they almost make it look too easy, just as you can if you give yourself an opportunity outside of school.

Let's say this out loud. Many of your teachers are frustrated by the rigid "lesson plans," tests, and technology that keep them from using their judgment and personal knowledge about you. They also know something you may want to keep uppermost in your mind: if you hold children to lower expectations, they will oblige you; but if you hold children to higher expectations, they will surprise you. You can demonstrate this all by yourself or together with one or two of your close friends.

Please be aware that I'm not going to write down to you, just as my parents never talked down to us children. They taught us by their example, and they quietly held us to high expectations, much to my benefit and that of my siblings. As you delve into these pages, get ready for lots of stretching exercises for the mind and notice how good it feels when you actually apply what you learn yourself.

Let's Talk About Screens

I'll give you some examples of these mind-stretching exercises soon, but first I want to address a topic that plays a large role in your lives. Even before the coronavirus pandemic studies indicated that youngsters your age were spending six to eight hours a day watching screens. That's a huge amount of time, and it surely increased when the pandemic forced you to stay home from school and use your computers and tablets and cell phones for remote learning. Without your screens, you wouldn't have been able to have any classes at all. Still, many students and teachers have expressed dissatisfaction with remote learning, for the simple reason that they miss face-to-face contact in the classroom. Perhaps your experience of being isolated during the pandemic has given you a greater appreciation for actual reality over virtual reality.

Remember, the internet is simply a tool. You can drive it responsibly, with a steady hand, as you would a car, or you can drive it recklessly. I am certainly aware of its educational benefits. It's hard to beat the web for retrieving information fast, but it's important that you leave time for reflection as you build your knowledge base. Without time to digest the information, you can fall into easy dependencies like relying on the web instead of mastering the material yourself. This is not the way to develop self-reliance and self-confidence and a rigorous creative mind that enables you to connect knowledge with action.

You'll have to figure out mindfully what's best for your own growth and happiness. Perhaps spending more time with others, including your family, will keep you grounded instead of alone in virtual reality, where powerful forces want to vastly invade your privacy, control your money, expose you to ugly anonymous messages, tie you up in click-on contracts, and sell you lies and fabrications about politics, the world at large, and even your own neighborhood.

It's been said that youngsters like you know little about history, the world, and your country, starting with your hometown. If that's true, perhaps it's because what you absorb daily from the internet and what you text about with your friends tends to be what's most personal to you, things like clothes, music, movies, sports, video games, and the like. That's fine as far as it goes, but it doesn't go far enough when you consider the vast world of information and interactive learning experiences you have at your fingertips, just by clicking a button on your laptop or phone, and all for free—that is, free except for those powerful forces mentioned above that want to trade your personal information for profit, as I'll discuss in more detail later on.

I'm sure you've heard it said that the best things in life are free, and there's much truth in that observation. Try making a list of what's best and free. You might start with sunlight, which is free and provides most of the energy our planet needs. Love, friendship, friendliness, and helpfulness are free, and you got your parents for free too—although in fact the value of what families provide their children in terms of care and mentoring, if measured in the marketplace, would come to trillions of dollars a year.

Can you add to the list of best free things? How about butterflies, birds singing their songs, plants that grow in the wild—blueberries, raspberries, mint, mushrooms, to name just a few. How about the wind, which can blow gently as a breeze or with force enough to be a source of renewable energy?

But what's free is not always good. Too much rain and wind can produce hurricanes and flooding. Too much "free" time online can lead to overindulgence and turn you into an internet addict.

Time Out for Gratitude

Do you think this line of thought is a good tutorial? I hope so, because it's a basic way of looking at the world with gratitude. The trait of gratitude releases all kinds of vital emotions that lead to better relationships among families, friends, and communities.

Have you considered being grateful to your parents, or other relatives who may be raising you, for all the work, money, sacrifice, and love they extend to you day and night? If you have a very narrow perspective, you may display just the opposite of gratitude, but as you grow into adulthood, and choose to marry and have children, you'll recognize more and more all the effort and time and nurturing your parents devoted to you, which may have escaped your appreciative sensibilities as a child. You'll recognize it because you'll be doing the same thing as you raise your own children.

In general, it's good to have a sense of gratitude in your everyday life. That doesn't mean you drop your criticisms or dissatisfactions concerning conditions or activities that you might want improved or eliminated. As my father used to say about love of country, "Genuine patriotism is being pleased with how far our country has come and displeased with how far we have yet to go." That was his response when friends or customers in his restaurant emotionally proclaimed such slogans as "America, right or wrong!" or "America, love it or leave it!"

Playing Different Roles Expands the Mind

All right, back to mind-stretching exercises now. Let's begin with what you call yourself. Who are you? Immediately you will give your name. Okay, but someone asks, "Who else are you?" You may say, "I'm a student," or "I'm a son or daughter." That same someone keeps asking, "Who else are you?" You get into the swing of things, and replies come readily: a baseball player, a poet, a reader, a biker, a runner, a hiker, a bird watcher, a video-game player, a painter, a big-time text messager, a babysitter, an eater, a sleeper, a gardener, a cook, an artist, a patient, a grumbler, a kite-flyer, a museum lover, a chess player, or (perhaps with some testiness) a test-taker. Your answers become ever more focused as you wonder, with some irritation, what in the world this questioning someone is up to.

Then the light dawns and you cry out, "I'm a citizen!" or you say, "I'm a shopper," and your nagging questioner says, "Yes, yes, you're an early payer of sales tax on what you buy. Someday you'll be a worker, a voter, maybe a juror or a candidate for office, maybe a homeowner, a parent, a caretaker, even a saver of lives."

By now you may begin to see the various roles you'll assume as the years pass, and you may ask yourself, "How is my schooling preparing me for such roles of living well and improving my community?"

There's another interesting thing about adding up your answers to the question "Who am I?" You learn to navigate different circles, or *frames of reference*, and your mind expands. For example, you may decide to start your day differently. Imagine waking up ready to plunge into a graphic book about the solar system and the galaxies instead of waking up worried about some nasty text message you received the prior evening. Two different frames of reference, each within your control to choose. In another way, activities like sports and hobbies give you frames of reference different from your daily routines. Routines do give regularity, focus, and stability, all good up to a point. However, too much routine restricts the frames of reference you can enter, thereby decreasing your new experiences and mental development.

New experiences can pull or entice you into a variety of frames of reference. If you've never attended a town meeting or city council meeting, it's not hard to add this local government frame of reference to your collection. You can read about local government, but it's not the same experience, is it? Actually, being there in the room, or attending a court trial or visiting a prison, makes additional frames of reference more memorable. More and deeper frames of reference make you a fuller human being with greater awareness of what surrounds you and affects your well-being and tweaks your curiosity. You're bound to do better in school as one result. For that matter, you begin observing more facts and fitting them into a pattern with various frames and a wider vocabulary that have real meaning to you because *you* shaped the pattern. You go to a store or mall and start thinking about your role as an informed consumer. You look carefully at the labels on the packages, at what you're charged or taxed. You spot warranties or quality issues and ask questions of the sales staff. Maybe you'll go home and download information about your rights under existing consumer law, rights that most buyers do not know they have when they realize they're being cheated.

    I suppose it comes down to letting your *mind* come alive, creatively and joyously, so it makes use of that wonderful developing *brain*. Yes, there's a difference between your brain and your mind; it's your mind that can decide how much of your brain you're going to use, misuse, or not use at all!

Concentration, Imagination, and Curiosity

Here are three stories that will illustrate more concretely what I mean. Isaac Newton (1643-1727), the renowned English physicist, was once at a social gathering when an admirer came up to him and asked, "Mr. Newton, why are you so much more brilliant than your fellow scientists?" The reserved Newton murmured, "I'm not more brilliant than my scientist colleagues, but perhaps I can hold on to a problem in my mind and concentrate on it longer than most." Remember the word *concentration*.

Years later, at another gathering in England, an acquaintance approached the remarkable artist and poet William Blake (1757-1827) and inquired, "Mr. Blake, with whom are you living these days?" Blake, never one for a torrent of words, responded, "I'm living with my imagination." Remember the word *imagination*.

You've probably heard of Albert Einstein (1879-1955), the physicist who came up with the theory of relativity. He inspired awe in other brilliant physicists worldwide, but he must have tired of their deference, saying that he had no special talents, just a passionate curiosity. Remember the word *curiosity*.

Can anyone keep you from employing curiosity, imagination, and a trained capacity for concentration, even in this cell-phone-frantic world? I don't think so, especially if you keep finding and developing various frames of reference that free you to engage these three central traits rather than immersing yourself in just one or another.

One life-lasting way to avoid such restrictive immersions is to query yourself regularly about your evolving duties as a citizen. Adults shouldn't tell you that you're too young to be an active citizen. Many children have found ways to help the poor, to clean a polluted environment, to invent things for the disabled, and to better their communities for you to believe you must wait to be older.

What If?

A great way to exercise your imagination is to ask "what if" questions. *What if* we relied more on solar and wind energy to save our planet by replacing oil, gas, coal, and nuclear energy? *What if* everyone who is eligible to vote actually voted? *What if* you could learn more about nature, not only in school but by actually being in nature? *What if* you and your friends could plant a neighborhood garden? *What if* you spent less time on the phone and on computer screens and more time with your family and friends? *What if* you collected real books to read and had more hobbies in the real world? *What if* kids ran for Congress or made up the White House press corps? This kind of playful but serious imaginative exercise helps you discover your own talents and possibilities.

Here's another one, a good one. *What if* grown-ups stopped fighting and excluding people and dividing people with hate and violence because of their skin color? *What if* grown-ups were more like us? We don't do that. We are a whole mix of kids and colors in school. We get along just fine. Whatever our skin color, the color of our blood and our hearts and brains is exactly the same. *What if grown-ups started thinking about people of different skin color like we do?* Daryl Davis, a black musician, was attacked as a youngster by a group of white people. "I was incredulous," he recalled. "My 10-year-old brain could not process the idea that someone would want to inflict pain upon me for no other reason than the color of my skin. He remembers wondering, "How can you hate me when you don't even know me?"

One of the boldest acts of imagination in our nation's history is the "I Have a Dream" speech delivered by Martin Luther King Jr. in front of the Lincoln Memorial during the March on Washington for Jobs and Freedom in August 1963. "I have a dream," Dr. King said to his audience of more than 250,000 people, "that my four little children will one day live in a nation where they will not be judged by the color of their skin but by the content of their character." A statement worth contemplating, among many others in the speech.

Social Action: An Urge to Improve the World

Let's go back to Greta Thunberg. When she first heard about climate change at age nine, she began wondering why so little was being done about it. Her *curiosity* impelled her to teach herself all she could about climate change, which she did with immense *concentration*, without anyone's permission. Once she had all the facts, she started where she could, with her family. She announced that she was changing her diet, eliminating meat and dairy, becoming a full-fledged vegan, and that she would not fly as a means of transportation.

With powerful science-based arguments, Greta slowly persuaded her parents and sister to adopt similar changes. Her father, Svante Thunberg, acknowledged in an interview that his daughter's advocacy affected the entire family. So compelling were her arguments that her mother, Malena Emmon, an opera singer who traveled all over the world for her career, now limits her performances to venues in Sweden. "I didn't have a clue about the climate issue before Greta got us all interested in this," her father said. "Once you start walking down that path, there is no going back. . . . your life is changed in every possible way." His words echo an ancient Chinese proverb: "To know and not to act is not to know."

Greta made sure that her family knew the facts on climate issues and that they acted on that knowledge. She has said that she is grateful to her parents for listening to her concerns and joining with her "to bend the curve toward sane programs in order to diminish man-made disruptions." She made sure that other people knew the facts too, and by the time she was fifteen, she was addressing the 2018 United Nations Summit on Climate in Poland, where she arrived by car. In her speech, she condemned the world's inaction in the face of the dire need to act. Speaking on behalf of Climate Justice Now, she accused her elders of irresponsibility. "You are stealing our futures," she said in a direct, no-nonsense challenge.

Around the same time, Greta's *imagination* was sparked by the young activists of Marjory Stoneman Douglas High School in Parkland, Florida, who mounted an impressive campaign against gun violence after a shooting at their school in February 2018 left seventeen people dead and seventeen more wounded; a month later, the students organized a walkout at their school and many others across the nation. Inspired by their example, Greta began her Friday strikes, walking out of school to protest against climate change in front of the Swedish parliament, an action soon emulated by thousands of students all over the world in their own countries. In 2018 she also met Jamie Margolin, a Seattle activist, founder of Zero Hour, a youth-led group working for action on climate change, and author of *Youth to Power: Your Voice and How to Use It*. In the foreword to that book, Greta wrote that getting to know Jamie and being involved with some of Zero Hour's marches made her realize that she wasn't alone in her concern for the fate of our planet. She and Jamie later testified before congressional committees about the need for action on global warming lest they and coming generations have no future. In connection with this kind of fear for the future, it's worth noting here that the American Psychological Association has recently identified a new syndrome: "eco-anxiety."

In May 2019, on Twitter, Greta pleaded, "Can we all please stop saying 'climate change' and instead call it what it is: climate breakdown, climate crisis, climate emergency, ecological breakdown, ecological crisis and ecological emergency?" That fall she arrived from Sweden by sailboat in New York, where she addressed the United Nations General Assembly, again chastising her elders for their inaction on climate change. Her challenge sparked worldwide protests.

Fifth-Grade Firebrands

Remember those fifth graders I mentioned earlier? Here's what they did.

One morning in Salt Lake City, Utah, a curious student at Jackson Elementary School told her teacher that she had discovered a dump near the school. She was not deterred when the teacher and the other pupils said, "No way," because they walked past the same site every school day. Staying cool, the girl insisted that the teacher and some students follow her to the site, a square block covered by thick bushes and spindly trees beneath which lay some junk and a nasty liquid oozing out.

The students and their teacher called on the mayor, who sent people to investigate. Lo and behold, it was an overgrown waste dump. The students were motivated to do something about it. "Clean it up right now," they demanded of city officials. It happened! Covered by the print press and TV and radio, the fifth graders, about ten years old, got lots of admiration from the townspeople and soon were testifying in Salt Lake City about a Superfund bill designed to clean up many of the worst toxic waste dumps in the state.

So inspired was the teacher, Barbara A. Lewis, that she expanded her experiences with her pupils into a book titled *The Kid's Guide to Social Action* (1991). Not long after that, she left the school and traveled around the country to encourage teachers to connect their classrooms with the community and involve youngsters in understanding how to make their community a better place to live. It all started with one fifth-grade girl's *curiosity*, which stimulated her *imagination* and *concentration*. What happened in Salt Lake City is called civic engagement in real life, or in a more fancy phrase, experiential learning.

Now to Chicago in 2004. Fifth graders living in a very poor part of that large city had to attend a run-down school that was crumbling in many harmful and discouraging ways. Heating systems that broke down kept the students in their winter coats. They lacked air conditioning for hot Mays and Junes. They had to contend with bullet holes in the dirty windows, broken desks and chairs, classrooms so crowded that some desks had to be placed in corridors, a gym of sorts across a busy road, a lack of necessary school materials, and much more. Their lively teacher asked them when school started what project they would like to work on. They replied with what was to them so obvious, with the fundamentals: they wanted to show how far gone their school was, to demonstrate the dire conditions they faced daily, and to agitate for a new school building.

As part of what they called Project Citizen, the students divided up their tasks, making a short video of the decrepit school and illustrating the case for a new building. They sent their urgent demands to the elected aldermen, as members of the city council are called in Chicago, and to the media. The coverage of their sorry situation in school caught on. The newspapers saw the kids as shaming their elders and the owners of those gleaming skyscrapers in downtown Chicago that the students could see from their shabby school.

In the end, they did not get a new school. Instead, the Board of Education sent them to a much cleaner, safer, richer school. But don't think these fifth graders, now in their twenties, are likely to forget that hardworking experience in seeking justice. To make sure they don't, and that anyone else who might be interested in Project Citizen can find out about it, their teacher, Brian Schultz, wrote a book titled *Spectacular Things Happen Along the Way: Lessons from an Urban Classroom* (2008), featuring the ten-year-olds in that fifth-grade classroom as central actors in his argument for civic engagement.

Winston Duncan got his big idea for change in 2005, when he was eleven. Visiting South Africa with his mother, Dixie, he saw an old woman walking along with a boy and was reminded of his grandmother. He was very close to his grandmother, who often needed medication, and he wondered how this old woman would be able to get medication, food, and other necessities. How far would she have to walk? "Why not give them bicycles?" he asked, and decided to answer his own question. With his mother, he started a nonprofit organization that refurbishes donated bikes and sends them where they are needed. People in several African countries have been delighted and relieved to receive more than eight thousand bikes over the past fifteen years.

In January 2019, Winston and his mom went to Puerto Rico to deliver four hundred bicycles to victims of Hurricane Maria.

It wasn't as easy as it might sound. According to the *Washington Post*, they had to collect donated helmets and attract enough volunteer high school students to help out with the fine-tuning of the bikes and to convey tips about bike safety on the island's roads.

As with other good charities, the givers benefit as well. Alex Wolz, a Wheels to Africa board member now in his mid-twenties, like Winston, said of his days on the island, "I don't think I've ever seen the spirit of community as I've experienced it in Puerto Rico. There is a feeling that you help people, you don't hoard food, you don't turn inward. You look around and see how you can help." Alex and the other Wheels volunteers learned an enduring lesson about how a resilient group of people responded to the massive destruction wreaked by a gigantic hurricane.

Peer Groups and Other Outside Pressures

As we grow older and pick up signals from our social groups, places of work, or circles of friends, we say less and less what we think about how we wish people would behave, or how companies should be punished if they treat us harshly, or generally why our society isn't better than it is. Less and less do we imagine an ideal world or say what's on our mind at any given time. This is called "self-censorship," and it's a way of saying or doing what will cause us less controversy, retaliation, anxiety, or hassle.

Thoughtful youngsters like you are not so heavily clued into these self-censoring straitjackets. You're more likely to speak out and wear your hearts and minds on your sleeves. This frankness may often be trivial or even mean and it may anger your parents. But when it targets public issues of importance, it can be a refreshing stimulus to an adult population that has too many marbles in its mouth. Remember Greta Thunberg lecturing her elders about ignoring the problem of climate disruption.

Did you know that scientists and mathematicians almost always do their most original, pioneering work when they're in their twenties and early thirties? That's most likely because their imagination and their curiosity have not been constrained by established ways of doing things, narrow mindsets, or rigid schools of thought where all the rewards are for *not* making waves, for *not* thinking in ways that upset or disprove past scientific theories or decrease prospects for grants to fund their projects.

So: delight in your present age. Take advantage of your freest years for exercising your *curiosity, imagination,* and *concentration,* while adding more daily experiences that are new to you and not part of your routine. If you haven't ever been to places your parents, grandparents, or other relatives like to visit, widen your horizons once in a while, break away from your circle of friends or your attachments to your cell phones and devices. Travel with members of your family and give yourself the opportunity to tap into their lifetime of insights, experiences, and most important wisdom, an all-important word you don't hear much about these days. Perhaps you can imagine my pleasant surprise, while reading the *New*

York Times* of July 19, 2020, to come across a column by Pulitzer Prize-winning journalist Jake Halpern. In it he describes asking his eleven-year-old son Lucian to create a utopian planet. Lucian took off happily to invent his own government and a set of laws he called the Consti-Lucian—"a fantasy of a world," his father writes, "where government and laws function properly."

Working more on using your age-related assets of idealism, forthrightness, curiosity, and imagination may take you down surprising paths that deepen your creative capacities. Once you recognize and use these assets, you'll be more sensitive to warding off much of what may be the narrowing conformity of your circle of friends, or the larger circle of acquaintances that sociologists call your "peer group." My mother used to caution us to "turn your back on the pack," meaning not your individual friends as much as groups of friends or acquaintances who may behave in silly, bad, thoughtless, and often self-destructive ways, not to mention the time and money they often waste. Here is one example you can use to apply thinking for yourself instead of going with the flow of your friends or peer group.

Until about twenty years ago, tattoos were almost never seen, except on circus performers and actors. You didn't see them on the arms and shoulders of basketball players and other professional athletes. Tattoo parlors were situated in the more run-down parts of town. Today tattoos are commonplace, and many people, including teenagers, are getting them on many places on their bodies, seen and unseen. Tattoo artists take your chosen design or words and etch them into your skin with a needle. The procedure is not without pain, though it's less than the pain endured when the person decides to take them off. After years go by and the skin sags, the tattoo doesn't look so good.

As a preteen, you may be anticipating getting a tattoo. Before you jump on the bandwagon, you may want to question tattooed adults, friends, or older siblings about what their tattoos mean to them. Are they showing off? Sending a message about their favorite sports team, singer, symbol, cause or image? Are they trying to increase their self-esteem, to go their friends one better by getting a more daring tattoo? Do they know what tattoos may do to their job interviews and pocketbooks? Many adults and teenagers reject tattoos. Use your own inquisitiveness, especially about why so many today, compared to the past, are induced to go with the "style," with the "cool thing" to do. I, for one, have always avoided anything that would damage my body, nature's amazing handiwork. Simple as that!

Order in the Classroom Versus Critical Thinking

There is another peer group that you may not recognize. It's found at your school, and it consists of teachers and administrators who worry about keeping an orderly environment and adhering to standardized rules and "safe" teaching materials. They don't wish to be attacked by critics who may think they are agitating or radicalizing your minds. But why shouldn't your minds be radicalized? What does that mean? Well, it may mean, for example, that you learn about businesses and their sometimes bad practices that cause pollution and other economic harms to your neighborhood, community, or country. At a Gilbert High School assembly in Winsted, Connecticut, peace studies activist Colman McCarthy was scheduled to speak about waging peace in a time of war. A parent approached the school's principal and raised a question about the legitimacy of the subject matter. "You have anything against peace?" replied the principal. So deep is our society into war-making and the military-industrial economy that talking about peacemaking becomes suspect and "radical," even though peace is the all-encompassing objective and desire of humankind and all its religious traditions.

While many educators say they like to get you into critical thinking, in practice they fear such an outcome. It can disrupt the lesson plan, take up more time than expected, embarrass the teacher, and upset parents when their child comes home talking about some controversial opinion, commentary, declaration, or criticism of the always present commercial interests. This kind of restraint on teachers is not what freedom means, is it? The famous physicist I. I. Rabi tells the story of how his mother would often say, when he arrived home from school, "Did you ask any good questions today?" That got him thinking all the way to a stellar performance as a scientist and to a 1944 Nobel Prize, got him questioning all the way to new discoveries in physics. Recognize the importance of questioning in your school classes. Gertrude Stein, a novelist and poet active in the early twentieth century, was once asked by an admirer, "What are the answers, Dr. Stein?" She replied, "But what are the questions?"

Teaching in the Cracks (2017) by Brian Schultz, the teacher of the fifth-grade Project Citizen class in Chicago, is a book that aims to help teachers navigate the waters of critical thinking in their classrooms. Schultz's example shows that at least some teachers allow for the possibility that classrooms should not be bound up with teaching you how to believe rather than how to think. Such teachers do not expect you to accept what is taught; they encourage you to disagree if you think the facts and what's right are on your side.

When I was a fifth grader, there was very little talk of critical thinking. A "good student" was obedient, a teacher's helper who always got high grades. One day we were told to read the story "Paul Bunyan and His Blue Ox." Paul Bunyan was a gigantic fictional lumberjack who weighed over two hundred pounds when he was born in Maine. He grew to be a champion cutter of trees in forest after forest as he headed west. His prowess lay in conquering forests, clear-cutting trees faster than all the other lumberjacks. When his small crew reached Montana, they decided to separate and go their different ways. Paul Bunyan and Babe, his great blue ox, headed for heavily forested Alaska where they would continue to work "until the last tree was down."

Was that the message that the schools wanted to leave me with on the last page of the book, me and millions of boys and girls who were told to read the Paul Bunyan story? Certainly that was the message the lumber companies wanted to convey.

They helped promote the myth of the valiant Paul Bunyan in schools. Children were being taught values terribly destructive to the environment and Planet Earth. Today, a Paul Bunyan book would not be allowed near a classroom, but the damage was done. Generations of students were taught to be indifferent to the consequences of clear-cutting forests into stumps for commercial purposes, including our public national forests. This *cultivated ignorance* in our schools, before the modern environmental consciousness took hold in the 1960s, gave the timber lobby free sway with Congress to obtain forest-destroying special privileges. Among these was the government-funded building of roads to facilitate the cutting of trees, for which the timber companies paid the US Forest Service a pittance.

Company Ads and Deceptions

For years, the cigarette companies, the oil, coal, gas, and nuclear industries were adamant that elementary schools were not supposed to educate you about their dangerous and costly side effects. The same was true for junk foods and pharmaceuticals. Over time, because of concessions to such companies, millions of students have grown up seeing the world around them through the lens of corporate advertisements purveyed on television and social media.

This is not a small point. Studies have estimated that from age five to age thirteen, youngsters are exposed to hundreds of thousands of advertisements in every conceivable medium.

Company psychologists and ad men are very clever. They often know more about you than do your parents or siblings, and they use their knowledge to make you want their products and entertainment, to make you buy and buy and buy.

Companies trying to sell things to consumers often embellish their benefits. Their advertisements may go from puffery to outright lying. The small government agencies that are supposed to police such deceptions—which can be very harmful to buyers, overcharging them or disguising shoddy or defective products and services—can't keep up with the huge number of ads. Think of all the ads you see in just one day on television or your computer or iPhone, not to mention newspapers, magazines, and billboards on the highways. These ads came heavily from the drug, food, auto, insurance, and banking industries, and worst of all, from what can be called the "addictive industries"—tobacco and liquor companies, and recently opioids and e-cigarette sellers that try to hook the young after many had avoided or stopped smoking.

Michael F. Jacobson, who graduated from the Massachusetts Institute of Technology with a PhD in microbiology, wrote a book with Laurie Ann Mazur, *Marketing Madness*, published in 1995. It's the kind of book that I would have read in my early teen years if I'd known a little then of what I know now. Food companies make claims to improve your health with products that are full of sugar, like breakfast cereals, or are loaded with fat and salt. The weight-loss industry has a field day deceiving vulnerable overweight adults and kids with all kinds of pills and liquid diets. Same for the products that sellers declare will give you sudden energy.

A notorious ad from a big drug company, Pfizer, claimed that its Plax medicated mouthwash "removes 100 percent more plaque than brushing alone." Totally false, so much so that two television networks banned the deceptive ad. Years ago, General Motors launched a national television promotion of its Camaro, claiming that the car had eighty-five new features. The Federal Trade Commission made GM tell its potential customers about all eighty-five. So trivial were many of them that an embarrassed GM didn't try this kind of deceptive bragging again.

Many books and articles have been written about what Michael Jacobson and leading medical specialists call "Ads that Kill." These experts tell the grisly story of how the big tobacco companies kept insisting that smoking cigarettes was actually good for your health. Even after the US Surgeon General, Dr. Luther Terry, in his historic report of 1964, said that cigarettes cause lung cancer and other diseases, Philip Morris, Lorillard, and Brown & Williamson kept *denying* that smoking led to cancer, respiratory disease, and heart disease, claiming over 400,000 American lives a year!

Science eventually caught up with these tobacco company devils. They were not permitted to advertise without clear warning labels on each pack of cigarettes. Daily smoking in the US declined from nearly 50 percent of adults in 1964 to under 15 percent today. Accurate information worked for consumers, along with powerful lawsuits that produced whistleblowers and documents from inside these companies, proof of evil strategies such as specially targeting women and children in order to hook them into a lifetime of smoking.

Drinking alcohol takes about 100,000 American lives a year and often results in drunk driving, family conflicts, and other miserable behaviors. The advertisements of the beer and hard liquor companies depict the good life, fun, sexual prowess; they target youngsters with images of adults enjoying their drinks with the children all around. The goal is to install the brand name of the beer into the minds and mugs of youngsters. These companies flood college newspapers with their ads and sponsor events with their brands all over them. The liquor lobby is powerful with legislatures and has blocked long-overdue higher taxes and warning labels on their products.

Since 1970 or so, ever larger portions of salt, sugar, and the wrong kind of fats have gotten into the stomachs of tens of millions of eaters. Over those fifty years, childhood obesity and related diseases have skyrocketed. Now we are told that 60 percent of kids are either obese or overweight! One in four children is obese. When I was a child your age, less than 5 percent of us were obese—but then we didn't have McDonald's, Burger King, and other fast-food chains delivering "tasty" gobs of junk into our mouths and down our throats, or supermarkets selling us the same unhealthy stuff. Back then there were very few ads directed toward us in an attempt to bypass our parents and sell us damaging foodstuffs; undermining parental authority was considered a no-no. Well, maybe bubble gum was the exception.

Now, all over the world, obesity, diabetes, heart disease, and high blood pressure rates are spiraling upward for hundreds of millions of people, both children and adults. A common reason for this is the replacement of local foods with highly processed packaged foods and sugary soft drinks produced and marketed by giant global food companies. A tragic example is mother's milk in developing countries, where ads push becoming modern and hip by replacing it with infant formula. Unfortunately, infant formula is easily contaminated when poor mothers add local water to stretch it out, a practice that has led to millions of infant deaths around the world, according to the World Health Organization.

The Dark Side

That's a pretty dark statistic, isn't it, millions of dead babies? Many grown-ups dislike introducing you to the dark side of realities near and far from you, as if you haven't already faced the dark side on television or the internet or in movies and video games. As a child, I avidly read the Nancy Drew mystery series, in which Nancy was the hero and the good always overcame the bad. Nancy is still around, in movies and TV shows as well as books, and she is still the hero, but her world is a little more complicated now, a little darker.

Did you know that the majority of kids around the world see and feel the painful realities of war, poverty, and natural disasters in their everyday lives? Here in the US, you may be lucky enough not to experience such calamities. You may have been able to have a real childhood, to enjoy sports and nature hikes, music and theater, puzzles and games and hobbies. And we adults want that for you too, but if we wait too long to tell you about the dark side of the world around you, to educate you about situations that can harm you, repress you, or exclude you and other kids everywhere, then we are the ones who are delinquent in letting you confront bad conditions for which you aren't prepared.

It's not just a matter of realistic education about what's wrong with the world. It's also a matter of lost opportunities to let kids your age make a real contribution to turning bad situations around. Consider the case of Joseph Califano, who was a top aide to President Lyndon Johnson and later served as US Secretary of Health, Education, and Welfare. A chain smoker, Califano was confronted by his eleven-year-old son—now a prominent head and neck surgeon—who asked how long his father would be around if he didn't stop smoking. The question struck Califano like a thunderbolt. He not only stopped smoking but went on to found the National Center on Addiction and Substance Abuse at Columbia University in 1992. He has been its chairman until recently, working against tobacco, drug, and alcohol addiction—and all that because his son learned about the dark side of cigarette smoking and put his knowledge to good use at home! Joseph Califano is now ninety years old and very much alive, enjoying his grandchildren.

Then there was the five-year-old boy who approached his father as he was sitting comfortably in his big living room chair, happily puffing away on a cigarette. "Dad, what are you doing?" the boy asked. "I'm smoking, son," the father replied. "No, you're killing yourself," said the boy, who turned away in disgust, fed up with hearing family members urge his father to quit smoking, to no avail. This curt remark shocked the father right out of his long-standing addiction, so affected was he by that tone of disgust in his son's voice! Out of the mouths of babes, as the saying goes.

Before wearing seatbelts in cars was mandatory, thousands of young children reminded their old-fashioned parents to buckle up when they drove. Somehow these kids had learned that seatbelts can save lives in a car crash. They knew what could happen to drivers and their passengers if they weren't wearing seatbelts when they were involved in a collision with a tree, another vehicle, or a wall. Boom, right through the windshield! The children may have acquired this knowledge from their older brothers and sisters or from their friends or teachers, or maybe just from being alert and aware of the world around them. Growing up with a grounded sense of right and wrong, a spirit of compassion, a grasp of facts and truths, and the willingness to question "settled knowledge" (for example, the alleged inferiority of women or certain races) is what changes the world.

If you are too much exposed to the dark side, your reaction might be to turn off or to turn inward, filled with dread, fears, and nightmares. Yet too little attention to these same dark realities may leave your generation passively signaling to powerful and manipulative forces, "Take me, I'm yours." What a prescription for endless bullying and further destruction of our democracy and our communities. Clearly, we must strive for a balance between these two extremes.

Maturity at an Early Age

Growing up takes place in two ways—physically as your body matures and mentally as your mind matures. If you don't abuse your health and you have enough food, exercise, and safety, nature takes care of the first way of growing up. As for mental maturity, that requires more nourishment, some of which comes out of your own experiences. In my family, when our parents had their friends over for dinner, they made sure we were included, sitting on the rug and listening to some fairly serious discussions. That made us feel we were respected for our minds. Learning to listen became an essential part of our upbringing.

The Harvard University child psychologist Robert Coles made a name for himself writing many books based on interviews with thousands of children. He concluded, in his words, "Children, young children indeed, definitely do possess a moral sensibility, an increasingly well-muscled notion of right and wrong, and, yes, a yearning that justice be done." You may become aware of this moral sensibility when you witness injustice, or if you've experienced a family emergency, a natural disaster, or, heaven forbid, a street crime.

In 1960, Robert Coles went to New Orleans to counsel a youngster who was the first black student to attend a formerly all-white public school in the wake of the 1954 *Brown v. Board of Education* Supreme Court decision outlawing school segregation. Try to guess how old this student was as you read her recorded interview with Coles, in which she recounts going to school each day escorted by armed federal marshals assigned to protect her from angry white mobs.

> I don't know why they say all those bad words. They tell me they're going to kill me, every day they say so. There's one lady, she's big, real big, who swears and swears. She gets red in the face. She might be getting sick, the way she looks. There's a man, and he calls me n*****, n*****, n*****; he just keeps repeating the word. Every once in a while, he says n***** *girl*, n***** *girl*! When I look at him, he starts swearing, like the fat lady. When I don't look at him, he doesn't swear too much....
>
> I don't know what to think about these people in the crowd. All I know is that the minister is right, when he says there is a Devil, and he's around, and you have to stand up and say you're on God's side and not on the Devil's side.... The federal marshals they have with me, guarding me—they're white, and they would probably leave me and join the mob, if there was a big fight.
>
> I don't want to fight, anyway. We're told in Sunday School to "turn the other cheek," and I know how: you pay no attention to the rotten apples in the barrel, and you keep reminding yourself that there are lots of good apples. My grandmother says that's what to think, and I try my best. I told her once that maybe there are a lot more rotten apples than good ones.

"You've just read the words," wrote Coles, "of a lovely, frightened, brave girl, experiencing each and every morning, each and every afternoon, the persisting, nasty, brutish venom of a vicious and stupid mob—and one undeterred for longer than was either necessary or just by a complacent, a blind, an outrageously short-sighted, narrow-minded political authority, that of the city of New Orleans, that of the state of Louisiana."

The student was Ruby Bridges, and she was all of six years old! Robert Coles worked with Ruby extensively and did not think she was a remarkably gifted child to produce such mature insights. You may have heard of her because she was in the news quite a bit in November 2020, the sixtieth anniversary of her desegregation of that New Orleans school. She still lives in New Orleans, and she is still a civil rights activist. Robert Coles wrote a great book for kids about her, *The Story of Ruby Bridges*, and you may also want to look up Norman Rockwell's iconic painting *The Problem We All Live With*, showing Ruby on her way to school.

What helped sustain this brave little girl every day as she walked past the screaming haters was the love and support of her family, as well as that of her white first-grade teacher, Barbara Henry. In 2020, Ruby published a little book in the form of a letter to preteens, describing her harrowing experience in 1960 and her later visits as an adult with generations of schoolchildren, to whom she conveyed her thinking about equality, tolerance, and love. Only sixty-four pages, Ruby's book, *This Is Your Time*, was her way of extending her hand through the years to youngsters of today and encouraging them to confront violence and injustice by speaking truth to power for change. "Don't be afraid," she advises, "This is your time in history." Hers is that reassuring voice that has your back.

In contrast, for pampered, spoiled, mistreated, or isolated children, it can take a long time to grow up in the United States, even longer than in many other comparable modern societies and economies. Historians tell us that in the Middle Ages, children as young as seven or eight were treated as little adults able to fend for themselves in "matters of the mind and heart and soul," in Professor Coles' words. They were viewed not just as economic helpers but as psychologically ready. "By seven and beyond," continues Coles, "one was supposed to know not to lie and cheat, not to disobey, not to get carried away with one's own whims and fancies to such an extent that one neglects one's obligations and duties."

Medieval society treated children as little adults as soon as they could work, as early as seven years of age. There were no mandatory public schools to educate the little ones and no child labor laws to protect them from terrible exploitation. Modern society, especially in the US, goes to the other extreme, allowing a long time for youngsters to be considered and treated as adults or grown-ups. College coaches regularly refer to giant football players as "our kids." The very terms "teenager" and "adolescent" were unknown in past centuries. Business created these identities or age categories to better target and advertise the products and services they sell. Treating young adults and teenagers as children prevents them from maturing mentally as they have matured physically.

When I was a teenager, the new magazine on the block was *Seventeen*. I confess I was surprised to have been singled out in this way. The magazine, attractive and seductive, was creating a peer group that did not help me in the maturing process. Rather, it pigeonholed me and others my age, telling us how we should look and think as teenagers. *Seventeen* focused on appearances and products we should buy, cosmetics, clothing, and the like. The magazine aimed to set standards for us. You get the idea? Again, as my mother advised, "Use your own judgment on presentation of self, and avoid the pack mentality."

Following the pack can delay your mental maturity and lead you to miss opportunities that you outwardly have complete freedom to take. Consider the story of a twelve-year-old boy I'll call James. He was getting good grades. He was a fine pianist and accordion player and swimmer. He was pleasant, helpful, at ease with people of all ages, and able to carry on a mature conversation. At dinner with guests one evening, someone suggested that he write a public letter to President Obama, who, like President George W. Bush before him, was conducting wars abroad that his administration and Congress did not want to pay for, as the country had done historically. James quickly realized that his generation would be the ones to pay for these wars as the federal debt ballooned, so at the urging of the guests, he composed a short open letter as follows.

> **Dear President Obama,**
> I just turned twelve and I want to ask you a question. Why aren't you paying for the wars in Iraq and Afghanistan instead of passing the cost on to our generation of kids. The newspapers say that all past wars were paid for by the adults

at those times with higher taxes. They did not borrow from their children and grandchildren. Will you send me your answer, Mr. President?

Sincerely yours,

James

At his age, James well understood that if his letter were put up on the internet, it might go viral, with perhaps tens of thousands of youngsters signing on or writing their own letters to the White House. They might write similar letters to their senators and representatives in Congress, in a preteen shaming of two branches of government. And the mass media could scarcely ignore such a news story. It has all the elements of children dressing down their august, powerful elders, who really could not find any answer that would pass the laugh test. People your age don't tolerate malarkey or balderdash (look these words up in the dictionary if need be).

As it turned out, James never sent the letter. I don't know why. Maybe the idea just sort of drifted away, or maybe nothing in his upbringing or his peer group or his pack made it normal to challenge the most powerful person in the US. Maybe it was too far out there, too off the wall into the unknown, too abstract to him, unlike the situation of six-year-old Ruby Bridges, who had no choice but to think maturely and steel herself against the brutishness she faced every day.

Semanticists, people who study the structure of language, help us by talking about "an abstraction ladder" running from the top steps of general principles down to nitty-gritty conditions at the bottom on the ground where people live. Children and adults react quite differently depending on where they interact with the world on the steps of this ladder. Perhaps James was too distant from what was going on, either on the ground in Washington or in the arenas of the two wars. Perhaps if he'd had a relative or sibling in the armed forces over there, he might have responded by putting the letter in the mail and posting it online. Or, more practically, perhaps he didn't think it would reach the president or that anyone would answer his question. Perhaps he didn't have a sense of the moral authority that youngsters can have on serious matters confronting our society.

I hope all this encourages you to develop your mental maturity and to examine your daily living situation. Let me stress again that you are a valuable human being to the people around you and even to people who may not know your name.

The Dictionary: A Door to Meaning, Understanding, and Enchantment

The more you want to know, the more you'll be thrilled to educate yourself in exciting ways as you bring into view the many-sided possibilities in your life.

I've got a personal story to tell you. One day at home in my early teenage years, I saw my older brother, Shaf, reading a large book in the living room. I asked him what it was. "The dictionary," he replied. "The dictionary?" I asked. "That's something you go to when you want to get the spelling or meaning of a word. You're reading it page after page?" He nodded. "Sure, it stretches my mind, and I find all kinds of words that relate to my interests, and I want to see where they come from. Of course, it improves my vocabulary. Every word or phrase is like the skin of a thought," he explained to me patiently, "a thing of history that makes you think and talk better because you have more words with which to think more broadly."

Shaf was a wonderful big brother and teacher; he really took the time with his three younger siblings, and we easily welcomed and absorbed what he taught us. Ever since that day, I have perused the pages of my own dictionary regularly. This habit of thought gives me enjoyment.

Author Jeanette Winterson keeps the twenty-four-volume hardcover of the *Oxford English Dictionary* plus supplements on her shelf. She finds in the *OED* more than definitions and derivations of words. "To me, a proper dictionary is a book of spells," she told a *Washington Post* interviewer in 2019.

The dictionary is one of the handiest tools you'll ever find for stimulating self-discovery and enlarging your conceptual capacity. After all, what else do you think with if not words and phrases that your mind connects in different ways? The dictionary helps you with that by telling you the spellings of words, their meanings, where they come from, and how they are properly used—all for free! These days you may think that you don't need the dictionary to check spellings because your computer does it for you, but your computer can make mistakes. Its fallible, even with all its algorithms and gigabytes—oops, look what happened there. Our computer couldn't tell the difference between *it's* (a contraction for *it is*) and *its* (a possessive pronoun for *belonging to it*). I should have written, "It's fallible, even with all its algorithms and gigabytes," but my computer didn't catch my error because both words are correctly spelled. Many writers, with or without computers, make the same mistake, which can only be avoided by wider reading, a grasp of grammar, and a sensitivity to the use of language.

It bothers me that so many people use words such as "kinda," "sorta," "like," and "so," often in short bursts with a tonal uptick that seems to convey a hesitancy or lack of self-confidence. What if I said to you, "The dictionary is kinda, like, so sorta cool?" Wouldn't you wish I'd been clearer and more specific about what makes the dictionary cool? A century and more ago, rhetoric—that is, learning how to speak firmly, precisely, comprehensively, and audibly—was taught in public schools. Now the overuse of words like the ones I just mentioned suggests that too much time looking at the screens on our TVs, computers, and cell phones has shredded attentive use of the English language.

Another subject that is no longer or rarely taught in schools is penmanship, the ability to write legibly in cursive script, or longhand. Many fine writers always compose their first drafts in longhand, including J. K. Rowling of Harry Potter fame; Neil Gaiman, author of DC and Marvel comics, graphic novels, and *Anansi Boys*, among many other works; and mystery writer Stephen King. They say that the physical act of shaping the cursive letters gives them pleasure, makes them think their sentences through more clearly before committing them to paper, and often sparks new ideas. Try it and see what you think.

To return to the dictionary, there are many fine ones available online, and you should by all means use them. They can tell you pretty much everything a print dictionary in book form can tell you. Still, you might want to take a look at a print dictionary. If you don't have one at home, you can find one at your school or town library (you may have to dust it off). Many print dictionaries today are illustrated with color pictures and graphics that make them very attractive, and they have one clear advantage over online dictionaries: when you look up a word, you can see all the words that come before it and after it alphabetically, something that can draw you into further exploration. You may even find yourself turning the pages in a way that broadens your quest for a single definition into a quest for knowledge.

Let's say that every day or two you pick a word you've just heard but would like to understand more clearly, so you look it up in the dictionary. That's what I'm doing now. I'm picking up my well-worn *Webster's Collegiate Dictionary*, my companion all through high school, and I'm looking up the word "freedom." Here's some of what I find: that "freedom is the quality or state of being free," as in (liberation from slavery, imprisonment, or restraint); that it can mean freedom of the will, frankness, outspokenness, boldness of conception or performance, as in freedom from care, and it can mean "possession of the rights and privileges of a citizen," or unrestricted use, as in "The freedom of my house is his."

Along with definitions, some dictionaries include quotations from well-known thinkers illustrating different senses of a word or different uses of the word in various contexts. For example, Cicero, an ancient Roman orator, lawyer, and linguist, brilliantly defined freedom as "participation in power." Many centuries later, in the 1940s, the social psychologist Erich Fromm made the useful distinction between "freedom from" (for example, freedom from tyranny, dictatorship, social conventions, police abuses, arbitrary arrests, censorship, serfdom, and other forms of restriction) and "freedom to" (for example, freedom to act creatively, to organize, seize opportunities, and employ the full range of our abilities).

Clearly, there are differences in the meanings of "freedom," and they are not insignificant, as Ralph Nader and others have often pointed out. In the US, for example, if someone asks whether you live in a free country and are free yourself, the way you answer might depend on whether you grew up in the inner cities or in the more upscale suburbs. But overall, you'll usually answer the question by saying, "Yeah, I'm pretty free." If by "free" you mean *personal freedom*, you're more right than mistaken. We Americans are free to choose our friends, eat what we want, go where we want, listen to the music we want, text-message whomever we want, marry anyone we want, use our money to buy what we want, play when we want, and so on. Even in dictatorships, although the people tend to be poorer, they are still allowed a lot of this personal freedom—if they're not in prison, that is. However, when it comes to *civic freedom*, that's where the restrictions tighten up on Americans. With few exceptions, we have few civic freedoms to shape our tax rules, our foreign and military policies, and when we go to war. Even the Congress has given over to the president its exclusive power to declare war under our Constitution. Our civic freedoms to sue wrongdoers in court and to engage in contracts as consumers have become increasingly limited. Did you know that we're supposed to have freedom of contract as buyers with the sellers we choose? But once you've clicked to buy something online, you never even see the long fine-print contract written in mysterious binding legalese that works to the seller's advantage, not yours (more on that later).

So when our rulers try to make us satisfied with them by asserting that we're free, why not ask them to explain what power we're supposed to have over them in elections and in how they govern us? As Supreme Court Justice Louis Brandeis said, we cannot have a democracy—a government "of, by and for the people," in Abraham Lincoln's words—and the concentration of wealth and power in a few hands at the same time. It is one or the other.

What did you think of this dictionary exercise in looking up the word "freedom"? Has it opened up many windows into a better understanding of the meaning of "freedom" than you had after all these years of hearing, reading, and speaking that word? Let's try another word, "justice."

A column by Peter Sokolowski in the *Washington Post* of December 19, 2018, caught my attention with its headline "Justice is on our minds. That's why it's Merriam-Webster's word of the year." Sokolowski is an editor at large for Merriam-Webster, a company that publishes a variety of dictionaries, and he explained that because their dictionaries went online in 1996, it was possible to tell which words people looked up most often in any given year. He identified two dominant categories of such words: "abstract nouns such as *culture, integrity, love* and *democracy*," and "words that spike for a short time, driven by current events." He went on to say that in 2018, "the word *justice* became the rare word that arguably fits into both of these categories, a familiar and abstract noun that never drops into lookup obscurity but that was much more frequently looked up this year than in the past. When all the data was in, it was clearly our word of the year: *Justice* was looked up 74 percent more in 2018 than it was in 2017." Sokolowski concluded his column with this thoughtful observation: "A word with broad meanings and wide-ranging applications inspired continued curiosity, and this curiosity says something about us collectively in 2018. *Justice*, in all its varied uses and functions, is on our minds."

Can you guess what Merriam-Webster's word of the year was in 2020? If you said "pandemic," you're right.

Grown-ups frequently comment that your generation has the shortest attention span ever. Some studies say this is because you spend so much time year after year watching screens where the visuals change in split seconds, even in more serious programs such as the evening news. If you look outside at nature, you'll notice just the opposite—how slowly the scene changes. In any event, if your attention span is short, the dictionary is a perfect fit for your frenetic state of mind, better than asking you to read an article or a book about freedom. The dictionary doesn't talk down to you. It gives you a serious, thought-provoking, mind-stretching experience if you just let it do its job.

Let's examine the meaning of another word, "wisdom," which isn't used as much in everyday talk and writing as it was in the olden days when I was a girl. My trusty dictionary says that wisdom is the ability to judge soundly and deal sagaciously with facts, especially as they relate to life and conduct, that wisdom is discernment and judgment, discretion, sagacity, that it's scientific and philosophical knowledge, that it's erudition or learning. My dictionary also gives me antonyms, words that mean the opposite of the word I'm looking for, and sometimes these give me even more clarity. In the case of "wisdom," the antonyms include, among other words, "foolishness," "stupidity," "rashness," and "folly."

To dig a little bit deeper into "wisdom," we can look at how it has been used in works of literature. I pick up another of my favorite dog-eared reference books, *Familiar Quotations* by John Bartlett, and find three to share with you. Here's one from Alfred Lord Tennyson, the celebrated nineteenth-century British poet: "Knowledge comes, but wisdom lingers." Makes you think about all the bytes of information you absorb daily and how to weave them into knowledge that provides the engine for getting to wisdom. A second quotation is from the ancient Roman playwright Plautus, who said, "Not by years, but by disposition wisdom is acquired." A third comes from another ancient Roman, Quintilian, a teacher of rhetoric: "Those who wish to appear wise among fools, among the wise seem foolish." You might wonder why I'm going back to ancient history and people who lived some two thousand years ago. Because the virtues and vices, the frailties and strengths of humans have changed little over the centuries, despite modern technologies, diffusion of knowledge, and a broader range of new experiences every day. The ancients had time to think, to ponder, to contemplate the behavior of other human beings and gain insight. They had no zillions of flashing screen scenes to distract them. To this day, they're very much worth learning from and knowing.

One more word: "intellect." This is defined in the dictionary as "the power or faculty of knowing as distinguished from the power to feel and to will, especially the power of reasoning, judging, comprehending, understanding." Going to Bartlett's *Quotations*, we find this from Viscount John Morley, a British statesman and writer: "Simplicity of character is no hindrance to subtlety of intellect." Notice that there is no mention of IQ, or Intelligence Quotient, that mischievous deception based on standardized testing. The IQ test was accepted early in the twentieth century as a yardstick measuring your innate or genetic aptitude to learn and understand. More recently, this yardstick has been criticized as preposterous and baseless, yielding scores more strongly correlated with a student's family income and living circumstances than with real smarts.

Being Smart

You can work up a lot of damaging anxiety thinking about who is smartest among the students in your class. Grades on endless standardized tests feed this numerical ranking atmosphere, and you yourself may internalize it by feeling less smart or smarter than your classmates. If "smart" means grades or talking well or reading fast, you should just relax. There are many other ways to be smart that mean more for your accomplishments in school and in life.

Some students are especially good at answering multiple-choice questions under time pressure. That doesn't mean they have any more intelligence, judgment, or knowledge than you do. Banesh Hoffmann, a physicist who worked with Albert Einstein, wrote a little book, *The Tyranny of Testing*, that included an episode in which scientists to whom he administered standardized test questions did not do well. Why? Because their insights into the science questions went too deep, costing them minutes and points.

Standardized multiple-choice tests do not measure the most important talents for success in life. They cannot test your judgment, experience, wisdom, imagination, idealism, diligence, stamina, and resilience, or even what you know about your classroom subjects. There are many biographies of people who did not score well on school tests but were great doers. They succeeded in their chosen professions and occupations, often starting new companies or citizen groups, inventing new creations, or becoming leading lawyers, writers, artists, and public servants. Never forget this point if you wish to preserve your self-confidence. The need to escape this trap of thinking that you're not smart enough or not as smart as your friends is quite important.

Multiple-choice standardized tests such as the PSATs offer very narrow yardsticks, and are coming under growing criticism from social scientists who think they're given too much importance or they're measuring the wrong things with their categorical questions. Youngsters who accept their test results may start limiting their own potential, thinking they cannot be biologists or architects or whatever they aspire to be. They may begin giving up on themselves because they did not "test out," and then they may settle for less in their maturing lives, a very destructive outcome. "Why not give everybody a shot in the classroom rather than focusing on achievement gaps?" asks Jay Matthews, a *Washington Post* columnist who writes about education matters. Dr. Warner Slack of Harvard Medical School has written many serious assessments of multiple-choice standardized exams and has called them fraudulent.

Let me offer you a shocker. You've probably heard about whiz kids in your age group who go on TV shows to answer hard questions. They seem to know just about everything—geography, history, spelling, literature, math, science, etc. There was even a recent TV show called *Genius Junior* in which contestants between the ages of eight and twelve were given ninety seconds to solve such math problems as this: 882 minus 632 times 6 divided by 500 times 12 plus 45 equals what? Remarkably, the winning contestant solved six of these problems in the allotted time.

Whew! Except that studies of similar whiz kids over the past century to see how they fared as adults produced more somber findings. Some who couldn't take the pressure and expectation levels fell apart psychologically. Others became good at their jobs but not spectacular. Still others led ordinary lives, with nothing to show that they had extraordinary abilities. Very few turned into memorable figures in their fields. Why? Because of three additional traits that matter greatly: character, personality, and ambition (or drive). When college graduates go to their class reunions, they are often surprised to learn who turned out to be successful and who fell short. Their class leaders, those voted most likely to succeed, most likely to come out on top, very often didn't, while those who did not receive their classmates' praise often did very well in their endeavors. The explanation usually came down to character, personality, and drive, except in cases of bad luck, unforeseen accidents, or illness.

The same holds true for youngsters with amazing memories for facts or statistics. They may win contests, but in the greater contests of life, the most capable participants are those with courage, moral sensitivity, a supportive family, and focus. The lesson is simple: aim high, but use your own demanding yardsticks and your own strengths to develop your potential, without negatively prejudging yourself. And don't forget that a strong desire for justice—some call this idealism—also sharpens your intellect, deepens your inquiries and insights, and expands your motivations. That is the smartest approach to fulfilling your human possibilities.

Harvard University psychologist Howard Gardner put a big crack in the narrow IQ yardstick with his well-received book *Multiple Intelligences*, in which he argued that people possess different kinds of intelligence, such as mathematical, linguistic, musical, and spatial. Beware of those who set the yardsticks in your life as you grow older. They may be good or bad yardsticks, but their purpose is to control whatever parts of your life they are measuring.

In sports there are clear rules (that is, yardsticks) that govern play and tell you what score you receive when you put a ball or puck in the right place at the right time. We accept such yardsticks as a way of improving our game—after all, it's only a game. In real life, there are yardsticks that measure (or do *not* measure) our economy, our environment, pollutants, the safety of our workers, child poverty, productivity, and the goods and services we buy. These yardsticks can be twisted, wrong, and manipulative. They can be far too powerful influences over our lives. Students who accept or are instructed to accept mediocre or low IQ scores as determinants of what they can aspire to in life's competition are selling themselves short. As noted, many of the finest lawyers, teachers, physicians, engineers, biologists, and other scientists had low IQ scores as children. Don't buy into this nonsense and give up your dreams of joining such professions. Ben Franklin, of whom you will hear more later, was arguably the leading scientist, author, business innovator, diplomat, citizen activist, and architect of early America. Regular postal service, volunteer fire departments, and free libraries were all his ideas. He had difficulty with arithmetic as a youngster. It was very good for our country that he didn't take an IQ test!

Solitude

In these pages so far, I've been trying to raise your expectations of yourself and urge you to begin teaching yourself in ways far beyond what you're probably used to hearing in your classroom. Self-education involves some calm self-discipline, notably in enjoying more *solitude* that lets you explore for yourself. Being overscheduled by school and family, and spending so many hours with your friends, whether online or in person, constitute barriers you will have to examine in a balanced and sound manner.

My parents had us children do chores around the house, and I became skilled in ironing my father's white cotton shirts. I found I could relax into a reverie while accomplishing this weekly chore, and it pleased me to take the job off my mother's shoulders. They also wisely left us alone outside with nature. I remember watching ants go about their business with an industriousness that impressed me at a very early age. We had our quiet time at home too. I can't tell you how valuable that time was for us, to tap into hobbies (one of mine was knitting), to read, think, and spend just plain reverie time inside or walking in the nearby woods. I so enjoyed the art of knitting and making a useful piece of clothing—a sweater, a scarf, or something more ambitious such as a dress. All you needed were two knitting needles and wool yarn. I loved choosing the patterns and the colors. Seeing even the simplest pattern come into view was exciting—completing a sleeve, carefully following the directions, developing a rhythm that came with practice. I remember rushing to finish a ski sweater for Shaf at Christmastime, anxious to knit an intricate black-and-white design flawlessly. That sweater still exists, and it was a big hit. Finishing what I started gave me great satisfaction. Once you start on a knitting project, you push to finish, and once you do, you'll have a sweater or scarf or hat that can last for decades.

Our solitary time was a time to "unlearn" as well. Unlearn what?

For one example, the myths or versions of history that we were supposed to take for granted in our classes.

History Infused with Myths

Since I was in grade school, the teaching of American history has become more balanced and accurate, but we still have further to go. Columbus did not discover America; he invaded America, seeking gold, and he killed many innocent indigenous people (he called them "savages") whose ancestors had lived there thousands of years before 1492. American soldiers were often just as brutal as any other nation's soldiers, exterminating many Native American tribes, slaughtering people in Cuba and Puerto Rico and the Philippine Islands. Slavery was far more cruel than pictured in the pastoral scenes on Southern plantations in our history books. We read many pages about the Native American "savages" and the "dim-witted" slave families.

Over the last fifty years, what students have been taught about Native Americans, African Americans, Hispanics, and women can be viewed as *unlearning* what children were taught when I was in school. American history was pretty much sugarcoated in our textbooks. Slaves lived on bucolic plantations, picked cotton, and had their own small houses. We never read about the violent brutality of daily life and the separation of parents and children sold to slave masters at public auctions. We never learned that slaves were whipped if they were discovered trying to learn how to read and write. Imagine their suffering.

Native American tribes sometimes offered assistance to Puritan white settlers, but mainly they were fighting wars against the white colonists for about two centuries. Like Columbus, the Declaration of Independence called Native Americans "savages." We didn't learn about the massive genocide against many Native American tribes, or about the forced relocation of many others that were driven out of their ancestral lands. For example, the Cherokees, who lived in the Carolinas, Georgia, and other parts of the Southeast, were pushed farther and farther along the Trail of Tears, so called because thousands of them died before they reached what is now Oklahoma—which was later taken from them too.

I didn't learn in school about the intricate Iroquois Confederacy and its political arrangements between tribes in what is now upstate New York and southern Ontario. I learned about it from my brother Shaf. Yet the Iroquois Confederacy strongly influenced the framers of the US Constitution and some state constitutions.

There remains much for you to learn about historical realities, often still mistaught, by using your intellect to unlearn what you falsely learned in school. For example, the Mexican-American War was not started in self-defense; it was waged to take land from Mexico. And your history books still called our country a democracy even during the decades when women were not allowed to vote and many minorities were blocked as well. I was never told in school that until the twentieth century women in many states were prohibited from serving on juries or attending law and medical school. Expanding the unlearning of myths that hide horrors is a major way of learning, don't you think?

The long trail of myths has consequences that are not benign. Those who fought for the slaveholding Confederacy in the Civil War and were defeated nevertheless glorified their rebellion, building statues and monuments of their leaders and continuing to promote segregation even after it was illegal. Presently, history is being corrected by the street protesters who insist that "Black Lives Matter," and Confederate statues are being brought down or relocated.

Then there is the so-called free market, which brutalized workers and injured and defrauded consumers. If you were nine or ten before 1938, when child labor was outlawed, you might have found yourself working twelve or more hours a day in a coal mine or a textile factory. Child laborers sweated in dungeon factories and mines. And how about the environment? The poisoning of our water, soil, air, and food began early in our history. Nature was to be conquered, forests to be clear-cut in the millions of acres. Democracy? Our history also offers many examples of stolen elections, rampant corruption in city political machines, and flouting of the rule of law. Countless documentaries, books, and eyewitness accounts have shown the cost of environmental, political, and workplace tragedies. Millions of people have paid the ultimate price for progress in the United States.

None of this should depress you. All nations around the world, many more violent and dictatorial than ours, are guilty of similar crimes. And yes, many of our renowned Founding Fathers of the eighteenth century had slaves and mistreated women, yet comparatively speaking, they built a democratizing society under law, albeit one heavily tilted to the propertied wealthy classes. What should dismay you now in the twenty-first century is that no other nation has had more resources, knowledge, laws, and successful pilot solutions to correct these and other injustices than the United States, but it hasn't done so.

I grew up being told in school that the US was number one in everything. Meanwhile, Canada and many countries in Western Europe were busy making sure they were moving ahead of us. By 1990 they had broader-based economic prosperity, less poverty, less infant mortality, higher average wages, and longer life spans. They also provided superior public services and economic security for lower-income people, the disabled, casualties of industrial workplace accidents (for example, collapsing coal mines), and victims of natural disasters such as hurricanes, earthquakes, and floods. Everybody in these countries has health insurance from the day they are born, which certainly saves many lives and catches illnesses and injuries earlier. Ralph Nader has identified twenty-five ways in which life in Canada is better and easier because everyone's healthcare is covered. Recently, Canadians added another. They do not have to worry that hospitals will sue patients for their unpaid bills, as vendors such as Danbury Hospital in Connecticut began doing big time in 2016 (see singlepayeraction.org).

Unlearning to Learn

For sure, there is much more to unlearn than in the areas just mentioned. In unlearning, we learn. In unlearning, we learn that what we were told for generations about oil, gas, coal, and nuclear power as safe, efficient, and essential, or what we were told about solar energy and wind power as pie-in-the-sky ideas, was not accurate. Such erroneous assertions were poured into our textbooks and classrooms to perpetuate the selling of these hazardous fuels by large companies eager to ignore renewable energy and efficiency. By the way, forms of solar energy were used two thousand years ago in ancient Persia, ancient Athens, East Africa and elsewhere.

Today you are getting more truth about ecology and energy than my generation ever did, but the darkness surrounding your classrooms has not lifted sufficiently to bring you closer to realities like climate disruption or to help you detect false statements and propaganda (look that word up for a real dose of self-education).

Our country boasts too much for its own good. "We're Number One" is a mind-set that is implanted in us at a young age. It's true that we lead in military power, the overall size of the economy, and taxpayer-funded development of science and technology. But beyond those areas we are far too smug, which is exactly the wrong attitude if we are to better our country, starting in the communities where we live and all the way to the national level.

My siblings and I grew up anything but smug. When we would

tell our father, "I'm doing my best," he would reply, "Don't say that because then you won't do better."

Too many people today who hold office jobs, often referred to as white-collar positions, look down on the work of manual laborers, even those in skilled trades, such as healthcare, homecare, and transit workers, mechanics, plumbers, electricians, and carpenters, people who get their hands and clothes dirty every day to make life cleaner, more comfortable, and sometimes just plain possible for the white-collar classes.

As a young girl, I was walking home once with my father when I noticed a man sweeping road gutters. "Oh," I said, "that is such dirty work. I would never want to do that kind of work." My father replied, "Because we dislike doing it, we should give him due respect and good pay for doing that grubby but important work of keeping the streets clean" (which is vital to public health). "Never look down on anyone or be in awe of anyone," he advised. "Just look at people, straight in their eyes." I can remember exactly where we were on Main Street, just past Richards Jewelry Store. I have never forgotten his advice. To this day, I thank people I see cleaning up for us in airports and in other public places. Thinking about what my father said helped my self-education in the years ahead, both in my course work and out in the world relating to other people. He and my mother, in different ways, gave me and my siblings a launching pad from which to figure things out for ourselves. They helped us clarify our values and make them more concrete.

Learning by Doing

In college, I read some words of the famous educator John Dewey, who championed "learning by doing," and they stuck with me. He said that education should "see to it that the greatest possible number of ideas acquired by children and youth are acquired in such a vital way that they become moving ideas, motive-forces in the guidance of conduct." I have thought of that incident with my father and the street sweeper as one memorable "moving idea" that guided my view of a respectful attitude toward workers. It's not that I was ever disrespectful, but my father's teaching took me to another level of deeply felt awareness and sensitivity. And there are many more such ideas to absorb day by day if you pay attention. A good habit to nurture!

Mr. Dewey was a very practical person. He noted that when your education is always geared toward the future, either the next school year or the future use of what you're learning, "habitual procrastination sets in." However, if you prepare for social life by engaging in social life *now*, you're more likely to learn by experience or, as he would say, by doing. Always ask education for what, learning for what purpose? John Dewey always kept his eye on strengthening democratic participation, once writing that "the individual must have the power to stand up and count for something in the actual conflicts of life." The logical extension of this statement is that when people do not stand up, dictatorship, repression, painful deprivation, and the downward spiral of community life are very likely to become an awful reality.

Toward the end of his life, John Gardner, a leading figure in public service, including health and education work in government, spoke to what some called the "contented classes" (upper-middle-class and well-to-do people). He was disappointed in their lack of participation in advancing solutions to problems of social injustice. In frustration, he left them with a question: "Who gave you permission to stand aside?" Wow! What a rebuke!

By now, if some of your teachers are reading what I've shared with you, they are likely to think that I am the one who's out of touch with *your* reality. I can just hear them saying, "Claire, don't you understand the different, difficult situations these youngsters have to cope with nowadays? Some are ill, physically and mentally, or their home life is impossible, disruptive, or unstable, or their families are impoverished, or they sometimes face street violence and crimes in their neighborhoods. As for better-off kids, many live on the internet far from parental authority or attention. Even if they were all well-adjusted, you're aiming way over their heads."

With all the pressures on them, child psychologists tell us, children are depressed, paranoid, jealous, rebellious, anxious about their weight, appearance, gender, race, or ethnic background. As a holder of a doctorate degree, I am familiar with the fashionable names that educational psychologists and psychiatrists have given to unfortunate and disadvantaged children—after careful research and testing, of course. These children are "obsessive-compulsive" or "introverted" or "bulimic" or "narcissistic," or they have "attention deficit disorder" (ADD), and on and on. My friend Dr. Martha Herbert, a pediatric neurologist who teaches at Harvard Medical

School, treated ADD children by showing them how to breathe properly, which quieted most of them down with no need for drugs, she found.

Some of these psychologists and psychiatrists are so sure of themselves that they break down the names of their asserted childhood complexes and subdivide them every few years. But as Robert Coles wisely noted, children have "a good deal of feisty shrewdness; a never-say-die capacity, in most cases, given any chance at all, to respond intelligently and with great agility to whatever stress comes their way.... [A child] who seems exceedingly troubled, at age A, may end up rather well off, psychologically, at age B." Well, that is reassuring.

Self-Education Can Be the Best Medicine

To the teachers who may think that I'm aiming over your heads, I say that getting youngsters interested in educating themselves and then benefitting from the self-reliant, confident, engaged attitude that follows can be a remedy for some alleged psychological "maladjustments." Your school counselor may have classified you as dyslexic, but you have other strengths, such as being good with numbers. You may be a good community organizer even if you don't do well on tests. You may be in a wheelchair, but you can still use your mind, you can still excel in school *and* in educating yourself. In a wheelchair you see the world differently; it's a "handicap" that puts you in a unique frame of reference. Greta

Thunberg was diagnosed with Asperger syndrome, obsessive-compulsive disorder, and selective mutism, which "basically means I only speak when I think it's necessary. Now is one of those moments," she said at a climate protest in 2018. She actually credits these "liabilities" with helping her stay focused on climate issues and feeding her unerring concentration on her mission. In 2019, when President Trump, a climate denier, criticized her in one of his incessant tweets, she replied firmly, "I cannot understand why grown-ups would choose to mock children and teenagers for just communicating and acting on the science when they could do something good instead." Trump was unable to rattle this teenager, and she had the last word.

About twenty years ago, I invited an educational anthropologist, Dr. Penny Owen, to come to my hometown of Winsted, Connecticut, to help teach social studies to our elementary students, some of whom had been classified by the school district as "difficult learners." Penny, who was uniquely skilled in instilling a desire to learn in all her students, hated categories and labels like "difficult" or "challenged." To her, the students all had different strengths and weaknesses, as well as multiple intelligences.

Penny—Mrs. Owen to her students—often began her classes by getting right down with them on the floor, sometimes head to head to help a particular child through a difficult moment. I have seen her begin a class by asking her students to stand up and shout, scream, jump, allowing all this mayhem to proceed for a few minutes before she stepped forward and said firmly, "Stop! Now we can go to work." With all that energy released, the kids could really focus. She broke through whatever was blocking their desire to learn, and they blossomed like tulips opening up in spring.

Penny has a background in theater, and she used it to stage Shakespearean plays, often outdoors, in which her students acted along with adults. She also coached them to play various roles in US historical narratives that illustrated how to solve conflicts democratically and seek the common good. She helped them find their voices, and they were off to the races. She had her kids singing and laughing and discovering both their individual talents and their common interests. They found motivation and self-discipline. Some of their regular classroom teachers who may have given up on them were astonished by their progress. Grateful families noticed that their children couldn't wait to get to Mrs. Owen's class each day. What a turnaround in attitude from dutiful to expectant and joyous! "She changed our lives," said one of her students who went on to graduate from New York University.

So successful was she that the school administration created alternative classes at the high school level for some of these students regarded as "difficult," and Penny took that challenge on too. Day after day, she refused to underestimate her students. Not surprisingly, they rose to the occasion. They produced a cable TV show called *Winchester Teens Talk* (Winchester is the larger town that includes Winsted), in which they covered three issues that mattered to their lives: drug use in families, foster care, and the alternative school and its effectiveness. The show won the 2004 New England Telecommunications Association Award in recognition of its quality and Penny's leadership in giving her students the opportunity to develop their gripping narratives.

Penny initially came to Winsted for a two-year stint and ended up staying for almost nine years. Her position was funded by The Shafeek Nader Trust for the Community Interest, so she was a volunteer as far as the school district was concerned. When she left, she hoped that district administrators would pick up on her efforts, but they were buried in bureaucratic problems, and so her grand project came to an end, to the sorrow of some teachers who had worked closely with her, and to the immense disappointment of many families. Innovators like Penny, educators who do not fence kids in by pigeonholing them in psychological categories, are badly needed in our country.

Addictions

Your doubting teachers may also tell me that I am not considering the addictions that are everywhere today—drugs, cigarettes, alcohol, vaping, sniffing harmful stuff to get a high. I say to them that these are destructive realities to be sure and that many were already common earlier in our history. But what about pointing out why many children don't get addicted as a way of better understanding those who are addicted? Could it be that supportive self-education can help overcome loneliness, anxiety, and a lack of the self-confidence needed to create a positive self-image and a transformed mind that enables children to develop their own fascinations and purposefulness as part of their regular lives? Youngsters over the years have shown themselves more than capable of such solid behavior, so why not now?

Addiction invites a number of external solutions—punishment, patronizing treatment, stern lecturing, regulations, the prosecution of drug dealers. It's true that addiction is a disease, but family and environmental factors can play a large role in preventing it from taking hold in the first place, especially at your age, when nothing works as well as the mind inside your head taking control and displacing the awful pain and despair that come with addiction. The deadly epidemic of opioids and painkillers claims more than twelve hundred lives a week in our country!

Finally, there is another addiction that teachers looking over my shoulder will want me to address: screen time. As I've said, even before the coronavirus pandemic forced many of you to continue your education online, studies indicated that youngsters were spending up to eight hours a day on their computer, cell phone, and TV screens. In all of human history there has been nothing close to any gadget that ate up so large a chunk of each day. My father and mother used to observe that much of the trouble kids get into could be avoided if they were put to useful work that made them feel like an essential part of family and community life.

Your anxious parents who grapple with how much screen time to allow you are worried about the quality of that screen time. Are you wasting time on trivia (text messages ad infinitum) or violent video games and other stuff that fries your mind rather than fertilizing it? If you are, it's like choosing food full of sugar or salt over more nutritious food.

Who's Raising You Anyway?

The ancient Greek philosopher Socrates used questions as a way to train and invigorate the inquiring minds of his students. He died more than two thousand years ago, but the Socratic method is still alive. For instance, it is used by law school professors to keep their baffled students on a fine edge of attention. Let's try it out on you.

When you hear the word "own," what does it mean to you? What are the things you say you own? Your bicycle, your cell phone, your clothes, your hobbies, your school materials, your computer, your books? What does ownership mean to you? That you get to control what you own, keep others from using what you own, loan or give away what you own, sell what you own, decide when and how to use what you own?

Make a list of everything you can think of that you own, all the way from pens and paper clips and old toys up to DVDs and savings accounts.

Now let's look to the future when you're grown up and have a family. What else can you add to what you'll own by then? Car, truck, house and land underneath, furniture, assorted tools, insurance policy, fuel for your furnace and motor vehicles, perhaps solar panels on your roof, your medicines, your food, kitchenware, oven, toaster, washing machine, power lawn mower (I like the whir of a hand mower over the fumes of a motorized mower and a hand rake over the environmental threat of a leaf blower), cleaning products, and so on—lots of stuff. By then you may have gone to college, maybe graduate school, in total as much as sixteen to twenty years of formal education. Lots of studying and exam taking.

If I continue to ask, "What *else* do you own as an adult at this point?" what would you answer? You might say with some irritation, "What more do you want me to list?" Well, let's back up and return to your age now to get a firmer grip on what I'm driving toward. What I'm about to say may sound a little heavy to you at an abstract level, but not when I go down the abstraction ladder—remember that? In your daily worlds of home life, education, sports, entertainment, communication, and one or both parents at work, *who is raising you?* You may mention your mother and father, your grandmother and grandfather, maybe aunts and uncles and older sisters and brothers. That's the usual answer, and it's accurate as far as these caring, loving, and providing members of your family go.

But if you consider with whom you are spending most of the hours of the day—that is, your teachers, your friends, and the companies entertaining you and selling you goods and services—your relatives are a shrinking part of your day in comparison to times past when youngsters spent most of their time with their families, and then teachers and perhaps some neighbors. There were few outsiders, other than the mailman, who came every day even before telephones, motor vehicles, radio, television, and computers were invented.

Now consider who has gotten their hands on your mind and body these days. By now you'll have seen hundreds of thousands of ads on television, your computer, and your cell phone, all aiming to persuade you to buy everything from food and drinks to clothes, music, movies, video games, electronic toys, pills, face creams, sports equipment, and many kinds of gadgets.

Given their success in enticing you to say yes, or nagging your parents to say yes on your behalf, don't you think that big advertising and big corporations are raising you with their products as much as, if not more than, your families (who, by the way, often don't see the advertisements you're looking at daily)?

I read recently about a ten-year-old who was creating an app (with the help of her teacher, who was focusing on the tool rather than the purpose) to convince her parents to give her an iPhone at her tender age. And she succeeded! The Apple corporation also succeeded, beyond its wildest dreams, overriding parental authority. And corporations will continue to raise you as long as you remain unaware of this *controlling process*, a powerful and helpful concept to young and old alike.

Come to think of it, more and more of what the traditional extended family used to provide for its children is now sold by businesses. Someone once said, "The Nestlé corporation provides infant formula, McDonald's feeds the children, Disney entertains them." There are day care centers that take kids in while parents are working, child psychologists who sell counseling, and coaches who push organized after-school sports.

Grown-ups who study this transfer of many family functions call it outsourcing to businesses what the family used to do for its children and grandchildren. What do you think happened? Economists have many answers regarding the "commodification" of family services, but the main changes were brought about by modern transportation and communication, which enabled family members to go far and wide seeking jobs. Distance breaks up the extended family of uncles, aunts, cousins, grandparents and in-laws. A more serious factor today is that one breadwinner's earnings are often not enough to pay the bills. With fathers and mothers both working away from home, more services have had to be contracted out, most visibly with day care, fast food, and entertainment.

Talking Back: Controlling What We the People Already Own!

As you watch television or scroll through your phone and see what the advertisers want you to use, buy, and own, consider "talking back," as Nicholas Johnson, a former commissioner of the Federal Communications Commission, suggested in 1970 in his book *How to Talk Back to Your Television Set*. You can begin by learning that you, together with all Americans, *own* the public airwaves over which radio and television stations send you their programs. Your public airwaves are regulated by the FCC, which gives out free licenses to the radio and TV stations. They control a slice of what is called the "spectrum" twenty-four hours a day and decide who gets on TV and radio and who doesn't.

Commercial companies pressured Congress almost a hundred years ago not to charge radio stations for these very valuable, very profitable licenses. Your parents pay more for their driver's licenses than the biggest television stations in New York City or Los Angeles pay for full control over *our* public airwaves.

By now you may be thinking, "Hey, if we own them, why can't we control what we own?" Brilliant question. Because the radio/TV industry has a lot of power over our government. It makes sure that it controls what we own and uses it free of charge. In short, the industry has taken the public airwaves away from us because we the people are not organized to take back what we own! If you don't like violent shows, or those that are just downright stupid and goofy, you should be able to complain to someone who might be able to make changes. Instead, your voice is shut down. I'll bet that many youngsters would like serious, fascinating programs on Saturday morning or afternoon national television. For example, wouldn't you like a program about inventors your age who have discovered creative solutions to improve lives? Well, there are a good number of them, but you wouldn't know it because the radio/television bosses who control what we own don't want to spend any of their profits to produce such programs. Cartoon shows, for instance, are cheaper and much more profitable for them.

Young Inventors and Tween Talk Shows

There are plenty of science fairs and invention contests for kids, but you won't see them on television. Have you heard of Gitanjali Rao of Lone Tree, Colorado? When she was eleven, she heard about the tragedy of lead poisoning in the drinking water of Flint, Michigan, and that got her thinking. She wanted to create a tool to improve testing for lead, so she invented a small gadget called Tethys, which when dipped in water has sensors that measure the lead content and send the numbers to a smartphone app that she also developed. Rao's invention won her the 2017 Discovery Education 3M Young Scientist Challenge, along with $25,000. How cool is that? Then she was named *Time* magazine's Kid of the Year for 2020.

Such an example should not be considered rare. There have been many contests for young inventors and many prizes for their inventions and discoveries over the years. In 1999, the Institute of Civic Renewal published a practical manual titled *Young Inventors: A Kit for Competition Organizers* by Yuri Huta, who wished to evoke the hidden imagination of youth and give their inventiveness an opportunity to flower. His section "Sparking Imagination" is designed to give kids "the techniques and assurance they need to think creatively." With his manual, you'll be playing on the same stage as adults who are thinking up inventions and making discoveries. (For a free digital copy of this guide, visit https://www.essentialinformation.org/inventors/)

How about the idea of going on TV with your friends to talk about anything on your mind, whether it concerns you, your school, your friends, your family, your community, your state or country, or the world? After all, you are part owner of the public airwaves along with every other American. Your audiences would be much larger and more diverse than your limited list of Facebook and Instagram friends!

Instead, you and the American people are kept off your own property by an FCC that has been co-opted by the media companies. TV stations may tell you that if you don't like what you see, you can hit the remote and switch channels, and if that doesn't satisfy you, you're free to turn off the set. How clever of them. They're tenants who don't have to pay any rent to you and all the rest of us Americans who are their landlords. This is how they're closing us out, and adults as well as kids your age are mostly clueless (good subject for a family discussion). Look at Saturday afternoon TV programs and ask yourself if they're showing you what's going on in America. Is this how you want them to use our public airwaves? Why do we take this year after year as television and radio programming degrades to curry favor with paid advertisers? Could it be that we never learned in school, even in college, what it means to own a commons, a collective possession such as the public airwaves, the public lands and parks, public waterways, public roads and bridges and drinking water systems, public libraries, public schools, and huge publicly funded discoveries that often build new industries—all paid for and maintained by the taxpaying people (your parents) of the United States?

Ownership comes in many forms. Without control over what we own, all kinds of costly, crumbling hazards and damage can occur. Your parents have probably paid for prescription drugs at very high prices, even though these drugs were developed with taxpayer-funded federal grants. Then our government, the trustee for the tax dollars we earn, proceeds to give away these newly discovered medicines free to drug companies that gouge consumers and patients. Pretty greedy and cruel.

You've probably heard capitalism mentioned favorably many times in school. One main principle of capitalism is that if you own something individually, or together with others, you should have some control over how it's used, if only to prevent it from being misused against its owners. Big Business ignores this principle even when it comes to making their own owners—the shareholders—powerless.

Learning about ownership in our economy and government, and thinking about what we own ourselves, leads us to a study of power and how a real democracy should be handling power. Going deep into issues of power and ownership throughout history "helps us address the problem of keeping knowledge alive, of preventing it from becoming inert, which is the central problem of education," in the words of philosopher Alfred North Whitehead. Do you know what he means? Just think of the hours you've spent in class and doing homework, wading into the stagnant pool of memorization to regurgitation to vegetation. Now think of my brief introduction to ownership and how you can apply it in your daily life and develop its meaning into expanded understanding. The deeper your questions go, the more your critical thinking expands. You see the world around you differently, more clearly, not just as a blur that may someday emerge to confuse you. You might want to take a look at *Land: How the Hunger for Ownership Shaped the Modern World*, a book by historian Simon Winchester, published in 2021.

The Importance of a Questioning Mind

Developing a desire and capacity for critical thinking has some immediate results. You're less likely to pronounce your classwork "boooring!" You're less likely to be bored at home or anywhere else when your observational powers are growing by leaps and bounds. A curious, questioning mind feeds those various frames of reference discussed earlier, which may help you avoid substance abuse, playing endless video games, and other harmful addictions. It is such a valuable attribute to be able to apply different perspectives and different contexts that can head off trouble, self-degradation, and excessive surrender to the pull-down pressure of your peer group. You become a fuller human being. Russell Jacoby, a historian of ideas, points out in his book *On Diversity: The Eclipse of the Individual in a Global Era* that group diversity is fragile if it doesn't allow for individual diversity within the group. Please pause and think about this point for a minute.

We live in a world of daily violence—wars, political repression, street crimes, natural disasters. Then there's domestic violence, which is usually taken to mean verbal or physical abuse of a spouse or child but also includes the self-destructive personal behavior of humans of all ages, sometimes called slow-motion suicide. We see this in kindergarten kids who demand food loaded with sugar, salt, and fats while loudly rejecting vegetables, fresh fruits, and grains even as they grow increasingly obese, which makes them vulnerable to awful diseases such as diabetes. You've heard about the bad things youngsters put into their bodies as they grow older, substances like painkillers that kill *them* along with the pain, or substances like tobacco and alcohol that cause debilitating diseases later in life, if not sooner.

Some of the brightest students at the finest colleges and universities engage in binge drinking—drinking alcohol to the point of losing consciousness or getting into other forms of trouble they'll later regret. Aren't human beings supposed to prefer pleasure to pain, health to sickness, strength to weakness, happy parents to desperately worried parents? Of course. But when young people do not develop their own critical thinking, they're sitting ducks for the instant impulse (often driven by commercial greed), the immediate high and gratification that come from slow-motion self-destruction.

A branch of critical thinking that deserves your attention is empathy, which is the ability to perceive and understand the feelings and experiences of others without directly having those feelings and experiences—in other words, the ability to put yourself in someone else's shoes by using your intellect and imagination. How about trying it with your parents? Can you empathize with them? Maybe you haven't considered how much they have on their minds in terms of work, paying the bills, and keeping the household going while they adjust their schedules to drive you to school, sports events, music lessons, birthday parties, medical appointments, and whatever else you may require. They do this because they want the best for you, but have you thought about getting the best from them? Let's face it, the talk that goes on between children and parents tends to be emotional, impulsive, and repetitive. They keep telling you how to behave or improve and you tune out. This is not a good outcome either way. If you can empathize with your parents, you might want to get to know them better.

Your parents have a lot to teach you if you only let them. What do you know about their occupations or professions, the work they do that provides you with food and shelter? I've met many youngsters who don't have a clue about what their parents do as accountants, nurses, lawyers, landscapers, salespeople, professors, plumbers, managers, and what have you. As young adults, my siblings and I were acutely aware of our father's economic situation when he had to apply for a loan from the Small Business Administration after the historic Connecticut floods of 1955 destroyed his properties, including the Highland Arms restaurant, which he wanted to rebuild. It was a difficult time for our family, but we were grateful for our parents' lifelong frugality, because we had some savings to tide us over. Such issues are usually not part of family discussions, but you can change that just by asking.

For as long as I can recall, Dad, a small businessman, would talk about his idea of wealth limited by law but with no limitation on income. In short, no one could pile up billions of dollars. There would be an upper limit on how much wealth you could keep but no limit on making income. At our dinner table with guests, he was in high gear. His limitation-of-wealth theory, he argued, would make the rich less likely to hoard their money and more likely to give it to charity and other fundamental good works. Because he knew that the political power of the wealthy accounted for much of their ability to retain their riches—through tax loopholes, taxpayer-funded government subsidies, and government research that very much helped to build most of the big businesses in America—he believed it only fair to adopt his proposal about the distribution of wealth as a way of helping many ordinary people and spreading the benefits keeping greed within reasonable levels toward a better society. That's what Andrew Carnegie (1835-1919), the steel magnate, decided to do voluntarily when he gave away his wealth to establish universities and over two thousand local libraries. Dad was ahead of his time in anticipating Senator Bernie Sanders, Senator Elizabeth Warren, and other voices now calling for a wealth tax. For an engaging story on this subject, see *Tax the Rich!* by Morris Pearl, Erica Payne, and the Patriotic Millionaires, published in 2021.

Family Stories

How would you go about tapping into your parents' storehouse of knowledge, experience, and wisdom, something you ordinarily wouldn't discover until you're in your twenties or thirties, if ever? Well, how about starting by asking them to tell you their favorite family recollections and stories? You can record the conversation on your smartphone, and along the way you can ask questions to explore their minds, their experiences, and their skills. If you do this with your grandparents, aunts, uncles, and other relatives, you'll end up with what amounts to an oral history of your family. And you might want to check out an organization called StoryCorps, which has been collecting stories from people all over the country and the world since 2003. They have a free app you can use to record your own stories and send them in to become part of their archive of tens of thousands of stories housed at the Library of Congress in Washington, DC. You might even hear yourself on National Public Radio, which features a StoryCorps segment every Friday on its *Morning Edition* program.

You'll be surprised at what you can discover and learn by opening a window into your family's history. It's an enjoyable way to develop your maturity by finding out where you came from in a connected way. Again, recall those broader frames of reference. Shared family history enriches the conversation with your parents and older relatives and lets them pass on to you many good stories, insights, and tested ways of doing and living—all at your own initiative. It's in your hands entirely! Don't delay if this excites you.

The concept of time has always fascinated me. Consider how often its passage is part of daily conversation as we ask whether there is time to do this or that. We can fall into a time frenzy: hurry up, we have to go, we'll be late for school, you're wasting my time, etc. At your age, you may be inclined to dismiss worries about time. You may think you have infinite time ahead of you and so you can be cavalier about it. My brother Ralph is acutely aware of the passage of time in light of how much good work there is to do. "Be Father Time Friendly," he advises. "Do not procrastinate!" He even wrote a poem about it, in the voice of Father Time.

> I am Father Time. No one can stop my realm
> All animates and inanimates are subject to my rule
> Animates more quickly, inanimates in due time
> No one can cheat me, no one can escape me
> In all the mighty universe with all its massive galaxies
> No one can turn me back, for I am relentless, omnipresent
> And singularly timeless, for no one can deny me forever
> I am invisible, irresistible, insatiable, unconquerable
> All I can offer you is my capacity to have you use me
> You can in varying ways, with many uses, use me
> And if you do not day-after-day, year after year
> Use me, you will lose parts of me that you will never recover
> Never in all the eons left of eternal time
> Because everyone and everything is mortal, except Father Time.

Take a reflective pause and allow your parents to give you their ideas about time, gained through their experiences. You'll be surprised what you can learn from them.

Remember Penny Owen? Her students were lucky because she had them interview their grandparents and other relatives and then turn their interview notes into a narrative of their family's unique history. The project certainly pleased their elders, and it made the students part of their family lore of storytelling, which anchored them in important ways as they matured.

Family Discussions

Listening to everyday talk between your mother and father is part of your daily growing up, but if what they are talking about doesn't relate to you, do you ever join the conversation anyway, just to know what their concerns are? Let's say your dad is complaining about taxes being too high. Why not ask him what he means? Supreme Court Justice Oliver Wendell Holmes once had an assistant who hinted that there was a legal way for the Justice to reduce his taxes, to which Holmes responded that he was definitely not interested. As he wrote in a 1927 opinion, "Taxes are what we pay for a civilized society," a point worth considering.

But back to your proposed question to your dad. What does he mean by "too high"?

"They're more than the family can afford," he says. "Who can afford them?" you wonder out loud. Your dad says the rich can afford them but they make sure they pay far less than they should. "Then what happens?" you ask. Your dad says that either the little people pay more or the government goes deeper into debt or it has to spend less for roads, bridges, public transportation, and other things that we can't buy for ourselves directly, such as public drinking water, sewage facilities, and public schools. "That's why our government keeps expanding its debt and is not repairing America," he tells you. "Just look around for yourself. See how long it took to rebuild the Wayne Street Bridge on the other side of town?"

Then you wonder why government's so squeezed, and why it's squeezing people like your dad and mom and not collecting a fair share of taxes from the rich. Your dad says it's not just the rich, it's the big corporations that give senators and representatives in Congress money for their elections, and hire lobbyists to help them avoid taxation, and get us small taxpayers to save them when they are mismanaged and fail. Frustrated, you ask, "Why can't we do something about this?" There follows a heart-to-heart exchange with your parents about all the problems they have to deal with, how the little taxpayers are all in the same boat and have to find ways to organize themselves and maybe meet personally with their members of Congress. You go away from that conversation with much to think about that never occurred to you before. I'll bet your parents will have seen a side of you that they haven't seen before either. That impresses them.

Talking things over with your parents and siblings will bring out the best in them. You'll find that you all begin to welcome some big talk in the family world of small talk, which at times can be trivial, petty, even demeaning. Imagine having dinner with your family for a week, absent cell phones, TV, and radio, and selecting one serious general topic to mull over. Let Mahatma Gandhi, the great strategist of nonviolent civil disobedience, help you out. Gandhi, to refresh your memory, was a major leader in India's struggle for independence from its colonial master, Great Britain, during the first half of the twentieth century. He spent considerable time in jail, where he engaged in serious reading and meditation. Long before the age of television, Gandhi became a soundbite champion of his time. He formulated what he called the Seven Deadly Social Sins. Each one has three words. Each one is a provocative and engrossing discussion starter. Each one touches on profound thoughts that you are quite capable of considering.

Here are Gandhi's seven sins, in his own words.

- **—Politics without principle**
- **—Wealth without work**
- **—Commerce without morality**
- **—Pleasure without conscience**
- **—Knowledge without character**
- **—Science without humanity**
- **—Worship without sacrifice**

In my own family, our discussions brought forth two more social sins to add to Gandhi's list.

- **—Belief without thought**
- **—Respect without self-respect**

On reading this suggestion of mine, you may be coming to the conclusion that it won't work in your family. What? Have dinner together? Not enough time. Too much yakety-yak from little ones who can't understand. Too many loud complaints about the food. Someone is always in a bad mood. Who can stay away from their phone that long anyhow?

Well, you're laying the basis for a small leadership challenge, aren't you? The first thing to learn here is not to prejudge outcomes, not to be too certain that a change in routine can't happen "in our family." Prejudgers are numerous among us. They rarely try anything new, rarely pioneer, rarely think afresh about how much more pleasant life could be with a few constructive changes. Why not take this up with your parents or grandparents or whoever sits down to dinner with you? Watch the expressions on their faces. You may well see surprise, a smile starting, a glow in the eyes, an expression of curiosity and respect. Besides, what's there to lose? It's not as if there's a downside. Nothing ventured, nothing gained, as the old saying goes.

One more thing. If someone reacts by dismissing political topics with "I'm not turned on by politics," you can recall your history lessons and reply, "Well, if you leave politics to others, think about those dictatorial countries where too many people were turned off by politics. Politics turned on *them* in violent and repressive ways."

Beyond Family Discussions

When you begin to talk to your parents, you may notice them doing things that prod your curiosity. Some children watch their parents fixing things, sewing, cooking meals, and show no interest in learning how to do any of these things. Other children are receptive to learning such skills from their moms and dads, maybe even older siblings. You can learn how to cook from scratch and make simple, delicious meals that are very good for you. You can start learning a little about plumbing, painting, electrical work, and carpentry around the house.

My brother Shaf was good at this. He once did the electrical work that enabled our mother to turn her washing machine on and off from the top of the basement steps without having to go down to do the laundry.

Such skills are often called "manual arts," once taught in home economics and high school shop classes years ago, before computers took over. When you're an adult and you look back on your preteen years, you may find such teaching moments at home very useful in saving you money and aggravation once you have your own home and family. Even at your age you'll find that doing useful work in your household is extremely satisfying for the soul, and that the manual arts require abstract thinking as well as doing, a point that Matthew Crawford argues eloquently in his book *Shop Class as Soulcraft* (2009). He offers many thought-provoking passages for you to ponder, as he does in *The World Beyond Your Head: On Becoming an Individual in an Age of Distraction* (2015).

Your curiosity could also touch on what local, state, and federal government agencies are doing that affects you and your family directly, and on the resources they can offer you. For example, the Federal Trade Commission, which polices deceptive sellers, publishes highly informative online articles to help you and your family buy or borrow wisely, whether you're interested in cars, insurance, clothing, food, or a host of other categories.

Then there's the wonderful newsletter from the District of Columbia Water Department, "What's on Tap." This two-page publication is sent to all the houses and other buildings in our nation's capital that are its customers. DC Water believes in educating everyone about the most precious resource on earth. They have online resources for students from kindergarten through twelfth grade on their web page, dcwater.com/teachers. This page has lessons, games, and worksheets about their watershed, drinking water, and wastewater treatment. If you've ever wondered when you turn on the faucets in your home, "Where does our water come from, where does it go, and how is it treated?" you'll find the answers here.

DC Water doesn't stop there. They have another page, dcwater.com/distance-learning, with dozens of online sites featuring "environmental education lessons, videos, and activities about water in many contexts, including health, earth, space and environmental science." Sure, they're based in Washington, DC, but these websites are applicable everywhere water is used and drunk.

Check out the water agency in your own town or city. What is included in your family's water bill? Here's an important question for you. Is your system municipally owned, which means the taxpayers control it, or is it owned by a corporation, which means it can set its rates to make a profit off the taxpayer? And did you know that your local water department is required by federal law, the Safe Drinking Water Act of 1974, to report to the public at least once a year on its water quality and the safety tests it runs on your drinking water? Why not request a copy or view it online?

"What's on Tap" seized a wonderful opportunity by offering science classes at home that can engage the whole family, including children who are taking their classes online because of the Covid-19 pandemic. DC Water caught this teaching moment beautifully and created an educational model for other water systems nationwide.

Discovering How You're Controlled by Companies

Thinking about your relationship with your parents and your family brings us back to the question of who's really raising you. It's a question we've touched on earlier, but there's more to say.

Most children don't like being told what to do. That's obvious from the crying of toddlers to the unruly behavior of preteens to the rebellions staged by teenagers. But outside your family, consider how you are told what to do or controlled in ways you never recognized. Just ask yourself this question: "How am I controlled by people or organizations and why don't I know about it?"

Well, one way to control you is through ads that lie to you. Companies sell you food that's bad for your teeth, your heart, and your health in general. No matter, they still describe their products as tasty and good for you. Drinks full of sugar and artificial sweeteners are advertised as giving you energy or making you look cool. A few decades ago, when smoking was everywhere, in schools, offices, trains, buses, and airplanes, the tobacco companies gave kids cigarettes as they left school in the afternoon, claiming that cigarettes tasted good and helped you concentrate. The companies certainly did not warn you, as they are now required by law to do on cigarette packages, that smoking is dangerous to your respiratory system and can cause cancer and other diseases. Lies, unrebutted by truthsayers who don't have the money the companies have, are a way to control you, to persuade you to do what they want you to do—buy and use their bad products. They addict you in the worst ways. Now, that's control!

Companies that pollute the air, water, and soil are also controlling you. You can't exactly refuse to drink water or breathe the air. Like many other Americans, you are a victim of what can be called "injurious compulsory consumption" (that's a mouthful!), a form of control that exposes you to the silent violence of pollution, such as pesticides, from which you cannot escape. A recent famous example, of course, are the children who drank water with high levels of lead in Flint, Michigan, and numerous other cities and towns around our country. Once you learn about these kinds of control, you'll see more clearly that violence is not just street crime, war, and bullying, which are pretty visible. Violence can also be silent, invisible, and accumulating, and it can shorten your life-span by giving you lung disease, cancer, high blood pressure, diabetes, and other conditions resulting from toxic chemicals, gases, and particulates from pollutants.

Can you imagine anything more controlling, day after day, than harming your own body because companies don't tell you the truth so you can learn how to avoid, diminish, or prevent these early corporate body blows?

For many years my sister, Laura, has taught a course called Controlling Processes to her students at the University of California, Berkeley, where she is a professor of anthropology. Students love that course, and thousands of them have signed up over the decades. Years later, many of them say the course changed their lives because it taught them to see what they never saw before. How? Because Laura discussed the real world around them in ways that led the students themselves to discover the controlling forces in their lives, such as their mounting servitude to gouging creditors, wrong medical practices, or landlords. Her students like her so much because she respects their motivated intelligence. Once the doors are opened to them, self-education kicks in and the experience leaves a memorable mark on their lives.

You can give yourself a simple test of how we grow up influenced to look at our country the way big corporations want us to look at it. Suppose I ask you what comes to mind if you hear the words "violence" and "crime." You'll roll these words over in your mind and come up with images of gang violence and street crimes. At least that's how high school students reacted when I and others asked this question. The students are not inaccurate, but here's the rub. There are far more *preventable* deaths, injuries, and diseases resulting from corporate-induced pollution, consumer product defects, hospital hazards, and workplace dangers, especially in factories and underground mines, than there are deaths from all the street crimes and homicides put together.

Now suppose I ask you what comes to mind when you hear the word "regulation." You'll probably be thinking of government regulation, but the truth is that there is far more *corporate regulation of our lives*—for example, in one-sided fine-print contracts, especially health insurance policies, or company decisions about the margin of our safety and health in consumer products, or controls for keeping our wages down or invading our privacy (think Facebook and others)—than there is government regulation. In fact, companies lobby the government to regulate *us* in their favor, or not to enforce the environmental, consumer, housing, and workplace laws that would safeguard us. One way of doing this is to starve the enforcement budgets of the regulatory agencies—that is, too few cops on the corporate crime beat. As for the cost of burglaries, hijacked cars, and robberies, it cannot compare with the megabillions of dollars that companies drain from us, as reported in major publications such as the *Wall Street Journal* and *Business Week*. Fraudulent business activities (e.g., crooked computerized billing practices) steal the income and savings of workers, consumers, and investors, all the people who nurture you, our children.

How about the word "welfare"? It's likely to conjure images of poor people on government programs such as housing assistance, energy assistance, and food stamps, but consider this. Most companies are on government welfare in the form of giveaways, subsidies, grants, and bailouts (as when banks and other corporations were bailed out by the taxpayers in the trillions of dollars after the 2008 Wall Street crash). Close to your home there's probably a major league ballpark, a football stadium, a hockey rink, or a basketball arena that was built with the taxes your parents paid to local and state government. These facilities are controlled by billionaire sports owners; ordinary people were not allowed an opportunity to vote down such deals in favor of their tax dollars being spent instead to build or renovate schools, neighborhood playgrounds, and other local recreational facilities. It's wise to know early that tax dollars should be used for necessities of life, not to enrich commercial entertainment.

The good news is that the billionaires don't always succeed. When Robert Kraft, owner of the New England Patriots, came to Connecticut governor John Rowland, seeking a half-billion-dollar taxpayer-funded stadium in exchange for moving his football team from Boston to Hartford, citizens formed the successful Stop the Stadium campaign in 1999 and sent Kraft back to Massachusetts, where he used his own money to build his stadium. But when the billionaires do get their tax dollars, they turn around and sell the naming rights to some bank, insurance company, or tech corporation. Shouldn't they at least be required to name their sports complexes Taxpayer Stadium or Taxpayer Ballpark or Taxpayer Arena? After all, the taxpayers paid for them in the first place. Isn't it strange that taxpayers almost never make such "naming" demands?

Good Companies

Despite what I've been saying, there are some fine examples of companies that respect the environment, their workers, and consumers. I hope you'll be as glad to know about them as I was. These examples show us the possibilities of responsible corporate behavior.

The Interface Corporation, based in Atlanta, Georgia, is the largest carpet tile manufacturer in the world. In 1994, its leader,

Ray Anderson, decided the company was going to reduce sharply its polluting activities and recycle as much as possible, including the worn-out carpets of its customers. The goal—to eliminate the company's negative impact on the environment and to take from the earth no more than they put back into it—was largely achieved in 2019.

You may have heard of Patagonia, which sells high-quality, rugged outdoor clothing and hiking/climbing equipment. They use organic cotton and all kinds of other environmentally friendly materials, and they require their suppliers to do the same, as well as minimizing the amount of water used in the manufacturing process. The founder, Yvon Chouinard, believes less is more. He even tells his customers not to buy new Patagonia products until the ones they have are worn out. He's also a great outdoorsman and climber of mountains all over the natural world that he works to preserve.

There are other companies, many still run by their founders, that belong to a group called the Social Venture Network, which is dedicated to building a more equitable and sustainable society. You can learn more about them online, and when you notice such efforts, you may feel better about your future prospects and how to develop specific criteria for selecting what you buy and perhaps what work you want to do in life.

Three Historic Americans: Beating the Odds Through Self-Education

Let's take a break from all these awareness exercises and journey into the past for some staggeringly different frames of reference. We will now turn to the stories of three historic Americans who overcame towering obstacles through self-education and went on to change our country for the better. You've probably come across these brave citizens in your history classes. Their names are Benjamin Franklin, Frederick Douglass, and Helen Keller.

BENJAMIN FRANKLIN

The most accomplished American of his time, and arguably of any time since, Benjamin Franklin (1706-1790) was one of seventeen children born to Josiah Franklin, maker of candles and soap in Boston. At the age of eight, Ben was enrolled in Boston Latin School but was removed two years later because his father couldn't afford to keep him there. That was the end of Ben's formal education, just two years of school. Everything else he learned during his long life was a result of his own diligent self-education.

Ben helped out with his father's business for a while, until he was apprenticed to his brother James, a printer, at age twelve. It was grueling work, and James was a hard master, sometimes even beating Ben for insubordination. It was not unusual in those days for masters to beat their apprentices, but perhaps less usual if the apprentice was a younger brother.

In 1721, James founded the *New-England Courant*, one of the earliest independent newspapers in the American colonies. Ben, by then almost sixteen, had opinions about what was going on in the colonies, and he expressed them in letters to the *Courant* that were consistently rejected. Undeterred, he used his imagination to create a character he called Silence Dogood, a middle-aged widow, and submitted his letters in her name. They soon became one of the most popular features of the paper, and when James finally found out that the author was none other than his younger brother, he was highly displeased.

Ben was a curious and voracious reader, often staying up into the middle of the night at a time when books were not as easy to get or borrow as they are today. Their very scarcity made him read them quickly before they had to be returned to their owners. In his famous autobiography, he said that he had a burning desire to write and learned how to do it well from his readings and from the conversations he had with older friends and relatives about what they were all reading. He loved to debate with his friend John Collins, another bookish boy, and that sharpened his language and thoughts and helped him retain what he read. As he lived near the ocean, he became a good swimmer, inventing what he called "pallets" that worked like swim fins for the hands.

Young Ben was very social, interacting with people of all ages and backgrounds. He may have been the most conscious self-improver of his era, carefully monitoring his use of time and what he did almost daily. He freely gave constructive criticism and advice as favors in his quest to become a better human being, always teaching others what he had learned. From ages ten to seventeen, his constant recording of his experiences and reflections laid the basis for the short bits of advice that spread to the whole world through his bestselling little books, notably *Poor Richard's Almanack*.

In his autobiography, Franklin wrote that he believed his brother's "harsh and tyrannical treatment" led to an "aversion to arbitrary power that has stuck to me through my whole life." He might also have said that what he endured and reflected upon in his youth shaped his life as did no other period in his amazingly productive eighty-four years. He repeatedly turned adversity into success and opponents into supporters as he widened his circles of fellow Americans working for the common good in our country and abroad.

At age seventeen, he fled his apprenticeship and ran away to Philadelphia, arriving there penniless in the fall of 1723. Philadelphia became his permanent home, although he was often away on assignments in Europe.

Ben was his own most spectacular and spirited teacher, a successful printer, tradesman, writer, and self-starting community leader who established the first free lending library, a college, a militia, a volunteer fire department, a postal system, and many discussion clubs. He was a man of letters and philosophy, an author, inventor, scientist, diplomat, statesman, and legislator, and a Pennsylvania delegate to the 1787 Constitutional Convention, where he made an eloquent closing speech.

Today, we might call him America's greatest builder of a democratic society, someone who never forgot where he came from and remained close to the working classes of his time. As a huge celebrity in Europe, where he was a diplomat during wartime, he met often with prime ministers and kings seeking his advice. Everywhere he went, people sought his advice, including Thomas Jefferson, John Adams, and James Madison, all highly educated men who had attended Harvard or Princeton. They valued his calm judgment and shrewd appraisals of people and conditions, skills they hadn't learned in school.

Ben taught himself science. He learned about electricity and invented the lightning rod. He wrote about ocean currents and plants and made other observations of the natural world. His curiosity was unrestrained. Even while sick and afraid during turbulent voyages of six or seven weeks or more between America and England, he would note in his diary how the Gulf Stream currents moved, affecting the sailing and the climate. So preoccupied was he with his studies and duties and travels that he severely shortened his time with his family, though he always provided for them. He was lucky to have a wife who adjusted. Unwilling to endure those interminable voyages to Europe on surging seas, she stayed home with the children.

Ben Franklin really was an extraordinary all-time beneficiary of self-education. His whole life was one of teaching himself, applying what he learned to real life and writing about his findings and insights for a worldwide audience. He himself was always proudest of his occupation as a printer above all the other influential roles he played, such as being the only Founding Father to sign the four major documents establishing our republic: the Declaration of Independence (1776); the Treaty of Alliance (1778), which secured French support during the American Revolutionary War; the Treaty of Paris (1783), with which Britain officially recognized American independence (so named because it was negotiated and signed in Paris); and the United States Constitution (1787).

Clearly, there are all kinds of reasons for delving deeply into Ben Franklin's productive and important life. For purposes of this small volume, though, I wish to stress that he had to overcome many obstacles in his quest to become his own best teacher. As I have noted, he grew up quite poor, one of seventeen children of a humble candlemaker. He had to save his pennies (remember his famous saying "A penny saved is a penny earned"), and he had a tense relationship with his brother. Life in those early colonial days was rough, involving injuries, sickness, epidemics, and impoverishment. Yet, driven by his desire to know and to use what he knew to widen his social circle and make things happen for the betterment of humankind, his curiosity never ran out of fuel. Just the opposite: the more he knew, the more he wanted to learn and to devise practical applications. He was indeed practical, right down to his inventions and his creative ways to repair what was broken. At the same time, he was full of philosophical wisdom that came in handy for everyday life. His practical bits of advice encouraging better character, prudent behavior, and frugality combined with industry (what today would be called entrepreneurship) filled his little books.

Where did these brief insights come from? Mostly from reading, introspection, and merciless daily self-evaluation driven by his aspirations. As a very young man, he would ask himself, "What good shall I do this day?" And by ten o'clock that evening, he would ask, "What good have I done today?" Impressive self-discipline, wouldn't you agree? Imagine asking yourself such questions each day.

Ben strove to elevate his peer groups when they succumbed to the lowest common denominator of superficial behavior. A born educator, he saw teaching as a way to retain and improve on what he had learned and discovered, and his pamphlets were highly instructive. His bestselling book *The Way to Wealth*, originally published in 1758 as a preface to *Poor Richard's Almanack*, summed up his thoughts about succeeding in business. Spun off into its own twenty-one-page book, it became one of the most popular books ever published; it was reprinted almost four hundred times and translated into almost every foreign language!

Ben projected great force of character in his writings and exhortations, which he tried to live daily. That's why he was so successful in getting the best out of people. He believed in freedom of speech, freedom of religion, and democratic principles. He dealt with facts and morals, with motivating people through enlightened self-interest. He did not shy away from social conflict but sought instead to mediate such conflicts for constructive purposes. He described conditions that needed to be improved in a way that was apparent to those he wished to persuade and mobilize "in order to bring them," in John Dewey's words, "to realize the social scene of action." Obviously, he was into fostering self-reliance, or as he put it, expelling "idleness, pride and folly." He never ceased to wonder about the world around him, and though vulnerable to bouts of depression, he worked very hard to get through them and avoid wallowing in that destructive state of despair.

Lest you think you've been reading about one of the world's intellectual geniuses from the get-go, take solace. Ben had difficulty with numbers as a youngster. As I mentioned earlier, it's lucky for him, and for us, that he didn't have to undergo a debilitating, confidence-shattering IQ test.

Ben Franklin did not pigeonhole his knowledge into specialties as is done today. To him, knowledge came as a whole, not divided into physics, chemistry, biology, mathematics, history, psychology, economics, and so forth. Unlike most people today, he knew from whence came his food, drinking water, and fuel, and from whence the taxes were collected. If he were alive now, he would inform himself of just how devastating are our modern weapons of mass destruction and our failure to negotiate effective nuclear arms treaties. Do you know how many cities one Trident nuclear submarine with multiple warheads can destroy around the world in an hour? The answer is about two hundred! Ben Franklin wanted his *brain* to shape as complete a *mind* as possible so as to link knowledge to useful actions. All this explains why I think every student should read his little autobiography *Ben Franklin, The Autobiography and Other Writings*, partly written in the form of a letter to his son William.

Let Mr. Benjamin Franklin command your respect and reinforce your motivation and maturity of purpose, your resiliency and enjoyment of the growth of your mind. His approach to life will stimulate you to follow your own stars as you embrace the quest for social justice on the ground and your own pursuit of happiness. Why not let this great human being, who knew his vices and faults yet managed to sideline them with his virtues and diligence, speak to you directly? Let him speak to you through his writings, with the wisdom of the ages and the example of a sturdy character that confronted immense obstacles and overcame them with a pleasing and practical personality. His writings epitomize the venerable saying that "the best things in life are free." Besides his autobiography, to absorb an added measure of pleasure, browse through *Poor Richard's Almanack* and you'll see why millions of people before you have done the same.

An anticipatory observation. You may be so overwhelmed by all Franklin did that you look at him as beyond emulation, like a Superman from another planet. Here's my response. Once Franklin achieved one goal, the next one was easier, or at least a step closer to being something he could get done, as in his diplomacy and his many inventions. He got better at things as his experience and the circle of those who respected him grew, and you can too. It's like honing a physical skill. You perfect one swimming stroke, and the next one comes like the next step. You learn to throw a fastball, and throwing a curveball begins to be just a little easier. So please keep that in mind. That's what growth and maturity involve.

FREDERICK DOUGLASS

Almost every history book in every middle school will have some description of Frederick Douglass. Why? Because, born into slavery in 1818, some hundred and twelve years after Ben Franklin was born, he escaped from his enslavers in Maryland and educated himself, becoming one of the most prominent leaders of the abolitionist movement in the United States. That's how great were his oratory, his writing, and his limitless energy in pressing the cause of freedom for people throughout the United States, sometimes in the face of violence. He even took his movement to free the enslaved people to foreign countries.

Until his death in 1895, Douglass was also a leading advocate for women's right to vote, which was not guaranteed until the Nineteenth Amendment to the Constitution was ratified in 1920. In the pre–Civil War period he shattered the bigotry of Northerners who believed previously enslaved people could never be as capable as he was in speaking, writing, rebutting, and strategizing for complex alliances across racial and ideological divisions.

In the years after the Civil War, Douglass became deeply involved in major movements for peace, land reform, free school education, and the end of the death penalty. His insights remain relevant today. Two of his most famous sayings are "Power concedes nothing without a demand. It never did and it never will" and "Knowledge is the pathway from slavery to freedom." Of all people, he would have known, because he endured beatings by his slavers merely for wanting to learn the alphabet so that he could read.

Put yourself in his place for a moment. "My mother and I were separated when I was but an infant," Douglass wrote. "It is a common custom, in the part of Maryland from which I ran away, to part children from their mothers at a very early age. . . . I do not recollect of ever seeing my mother by the light of day.... She would lie down with me, and get me to sleep, but long before I waked she was gone." Young Frederick only saw his mother four or five times, on her secret nocturnal visits from a distant farm to which she was sold when he was a baby. He didn't know who his father was, only that he was a white master. It's hard to imagine being enslaved as a child, worked to the bone without the nurturing and shielding of parents, subjected to or seeing horrific punishments and violations inflicted by the slaveholder and his goons. Day after day, night after night, on plantations large and small, slave owners and their overseers would whip women into bloody pulps when they were not raping them. Slavery meant there were no laws to prevent total domination. Enslaved people had to gauge the relative brutality of their masters to determine what degree of restraint they could expect.

In a letter introducing *Narrative of the Life of Frederick Douglass, An American Slave, Written by Himself* (the first of three autobiographies), Boston abolitionist Wendell Phillips wrote, addressing Douglass directly, "I was glad to learn, in your story, how early the most neglected of God's children waken to a sense of their rights, and of the injustice done them. Experience is a keen teacher; and long before you had mastered your A B C, ... you began, I see, to gauge the wretchedness of the slave, not by his hunger and want, not by his lashes and toil, but by the cruel and blighting death which gathers over his soul." It was an elegant way of saying that Douglass began thinking deeply *before* he began his furtive efforts to learn his ABCs.

In his preface to the same book, another prominent abolitionist, William Lloyd Garrison, wrote "of cruel scourgings, of mutilations and brandings, of scenes of pollution and blood, of the banishment of all light and knowledge ... [of] whips, chains, thumb-screws, paddles, blood-hounds, overseers, drivers, patrols ... [of] concubinage, adultery, and incest." Only in recent years have white Americans and their children been exposed to the savagery of slavery in popular films like *Twelve Years a Slave* and in documentaries and books. My textbooks in the 1940s glossed over this violent criminal period in our history, depicting happy enslaved families in idyllic plantation scenes. Similarly, my textbooks ignored the genocide of Native American tribes.

Passed from one slaveholder to another, Frederick was "given" to Hugh and Sophia Auld of Baltimore at age seven or eight. Life as an enslaved person in the city was not as harsh as it would have been on a rural plantation once he was old enough to work in the fields. Mrs. Auld, he tells us, "very kindly commenced to teach me the A B C. After I had learned this, she assisted me in learning to spell words of three or four letters. Just at this point of my progress, Mr. Auld found out what was going on, and at once forbade Mrs. Auld to instruct me further, telling her, among other things, that it was unlawful, as well as unsafe, to teach a slave to read. [He said,] 'A n***** should know nothing but to obey his master—to do as he is told to do. Learning would *spoil* the best n***** in the world. . . . It would make him discontented and unhappy.'" Douglass wrote that Mr. Auld's words "sank deep into my heart. . . . From that moment, I understood the pathway from slavery to freedom. . . . Though conscious of the difficulty of learning without a teacher, I set out with high hope, and a fixed purpose, at whatever cost of trouble, to learn how to read."

Frederick stayed with the Auld family for about seven years, during which he secretly taught himself to read and write, taking care not to be caught with a newspaper or a pamphlet lest his owners inflict harsh punishment. By now, dear reader, you might be engaged in a wondering comparison with your own free state of mind and learning.

Thanks to Mrs. Auld, Frederick knew his alphabet, but he still couldn't read. How did he learn? "The plan which I adopted, and the one by which I was most successful, was that of making friends of all the little white boys whom I met in the street. As many of these as I could, I converted into teachers." In the Auld household, Frederick was allowed to have as much bread as he wanted, and when he was sent on errands, he would take some with him, along with a book he carried surreptitiously. The white children in his neighborhood were often from poor families, but they had some schooling, so he offered a trade: bread for a reading lesson. "This bread I used to bestow upon the hungry little urchins, who, in return, would give me that more valuable bread of knowledge."

Soon he strove to teach himself how to write. He was often sent to a local shipyard, where he saw carpenters writing letters on the various timbers of the ship they were building: S if the timber was meant to go on the ship's starboard side, L for the larboard side, A for aft, F for forward. "I soon learned the names of these letters, and for what they were intended when placed upon a piece of timber in the ship-yard," he tells us. "I immediately commenced copying them, and in a short time was able to make the four letters named. After that, when I met with any boy who I knew could write, I would tell him I could write as well as he." Of course the boy would challenge him to prove it, and after Frederick formed his four letters, the boy would outdo him. "In this way I got a good many lessons in writing, which it is quite possible I should never have gotten in any other way. During this time, my copy-book was the board fence, brick wall, and pavement; my pen and ink was a lump of chalk." Thus, step by torturous step, letter by difficult letter, young Frederick taught himself to write.

In 1834, just shy of his sixteenth birthday, and after some bitter experiences with cruel masters, Frederick was hired out to William Freedland, who owned just two slaves, Henry Harris and John Harris, but employed several others who were hired out like Frederick. "Henry and John were quite intelligent," he writes, "and in a very little while after I went there, I succeeded in creating in them a strong desire to learn how to read. This desire soon sprang up in the others also. They very soon mustered up some old spelling-books, and nothing would do but that I must keep a Sabbath school. I agreed to do so, and accordingly devoted my Sundays to teaching these my loved fellow-slaves how to read. . . . Some of the slaves of the neighboring farms found what was going on, and also availed themselves of this little opportunity to learn to read."

Frederick held his Sabbath school "at the house of a free colored man, whose name I deem it imprudent to mention." In addition, he spent three evenings a week teaching slaves at home. On one occasion, plantation owners who had found out about the secret school "rushed in upon us with sticks and stones." Nevertheless, Frederick persisted, and as he taught others rudimentary reading, he became a more proficient reader himself, not to mention "the delight of my soul to be doing something that looked like bettering the condition of my race" and giving them a pathway to freedom.

In September 1838, Frederick escaped from slavery. "I left my chains, and succeeded in reaching New York," he wrote, but gave no details for fear of endangering those who had helped him. He spent three years as a manual laborer, during which time he became a close reader of the *Liberator*, an abolitionist newspaper, and embarked on his career as a public speaker and writer, who championed the cause of ending the curse of slavery, to wide recognition. He enjoyed adulation but also endured ugly denunciations and threats of physical harm as he lived a spectacular embodiment of his core belief that knowledge is the pathway from slavery to freedom.

In his later years, Douglass frequently mentioned an anthology, *The Colombian Orator*, that he discovered when he was twelve. This book, published in 1797, was a classroom reader containing many anti-slavery speeches, essays, and conversations that he devoured to improve his grammar and reading capacity, and to strengthen his commitment to human rights, freedom, and justice. It was just as his slaveholders feared, which further intensified his motivation to prove them right. You might want to compare the difficulties you're facing in your studies with those of Frederick Douglass. Thinking about his story as a formerly enslaved person, and the staggering amount of grit he showed to overcome his brutal circumstances, might leave you feeling inspired. Frederick Douglass remains, however many years later, a beacon, and a reminder that you can rise to the occasions that beckon you. As the renowned twentieth-century American poet Robert Frost said, "The best way out is always through."

HELEN KELLER

Born in Tuscumbia, Alabama, in 1880, Helen Keller became one of the best-known women of the twentieth century. By the time she died in 1968, she was admired all over the world for her inspiring life and her advocacy for justice and peace. In her numerous books, articles, and interviews, in her worldwide visits to powerful decision-makers, leading thinkers, inventors, and physicians, in her speeches before large assemblies, she fought for the rights of exploited workers, for women's right to vote, for people with disabilities, and against repressive economic and political institutions. Movies, documentaries, and stage plays recounted her enduring achievement.

Would it astonish you to learn that this remarkable woman, as a nineteen-month-old infant, was afflicted with an unknown illness, maybe scarlet fever or meningitis, and rendered *blind and deaf*? Suddenly little Helen could not see, hear, or speak. What she did retain was a good brain, a mind of endless curiosity, and a sense of touch and smell that became sharper as time passed. Around her homestead, she learned to identify who was walking by from the vibrations of their footsteps. She used rough homemade signs to communicate a little with Martha Washington, who was two or three years older and the daughter of the family cook.

Time for some extraordinary empathy. Put yourself in Helen's situation at age six when her adoring mother read about Laura Bridgman, a deaf and blind woman whose successful education was described in Charles Dickens' *American Notes*. Mrs. Keller's further searches led her to Alexander Graham Bell, known not only for inventing the telephone but for his work with deaf children. Bell referred her to the Perkins Institute for the Blind in Boston, where Laura Bridgman had been a student. There she found another former student, Anne Sullivan, who agreed to come to Alabama and become Helen's full-time instructor and governess. This historic relationship lasted for forty-nine years!

At Helen's age, what would you have been thinking about in your dark, silent world? How could your mother and father know that you wanted someone to work with you as a full-time teacher? Helen had no motivational difficulty; she was curious, frisky, always ready to play with other children and fearlessly run through the gardens without any self-pity or moroseness. Most of the time she was upbeat, even feisty, probably in part because she could not remember a time when she wasn't blind and deaf. Helen couldn't know that she and Miss Sullivan, as she always called her teacher, were embarking on a historic experiment that was to catch the attention of millions the world over who were working with the disabled and striving to overcome the exclusion, the marginalization, the patronizing of people with physical disabilities.

And Helen's parents, Kate Adams Keller and Arthur Keller, were not expecting any historic breakthroughs; they merely wanted the best possible care and education for their firstborn child.

What regular children took for granted, Helen had to move forward inch by inch through excruciating practice, over and over again. She had one advantage in that everything she learned to do she instantly incorporated into her physical and mental development in preparation for the next step up the ladder. There was no problem of lack of interest. I'm sure Alfred North Whitehead's words were never truer for Helen than when he wrote, "Unless the pupils are continually sustained by the evocation of interest, the acquirement of technique, and the excitement of success, they can never make progress, and will certainly lose heart."

I invited your empathy a moment ago, but it's doubtful that you or anyone else could empathize with the loss of all three major human faculties of communication. How would we know where and how to begin the improbable journey to comparable functions in the face of permanent loss of the original senses?

In the years after her illness, Helen showed her determination, as well as her temper and frustrations. Writing in her autobiography *The Story of My Life*, published when she was twenty-two, Helen had this to say about those years:

> **My hands felt every object and observed every motion, and in this way I learned to know many things. Soon I . . . began to make crude signs. A shake of the head meant "No" and a nod, "Yes," a pull meant "Come" and a push, "Go." Was it bread that**

> I wanted? Then I would imitate the acts of cutting the slices and buttering them. . . . My mother, moreover, succeeded in making me understand a good deal. I always knew when she wished me to bring her something, and I would run upstairs or anywhere else she indicated. Indeed, I owe to her loving wisdom all that was bright and good in my long night. . . . At five I learned to fold and put away the clean clothes when they were brought in from the laundry, and I distinguished my own from the rest.

But there was always the haunting darkness from the closure of the eyes, the ears, and the voice. Here is Helen again.

> I do not remember when I first realized that I was different from other people, but I knew it before my teacher came to me. I had noticed that my mother and my friends did not use signs as I did when they wanted anything done, but talked with their mouths. Sometimes I stood between two persons who were conversing and touched their lips. I could not understand, and was vexed. I moved my lips and gesticulated frantically without result. This made me so angry at times that I kicked and screamed until I was exhausted.

Helen was approaching the age when most children enter kindergarten. About her attitude then, she wrote, "The desire to express myself grew. The few signs I used became less and less adequate, and my failures to make myself understood were invariably followed by outbursts of passion. I felt as if invisible hands were holding me, and I made frantic efforts to free myself. I struggled—not that struggling helped matters, but the spirit of resistance was strong within me."

We can see Helen's amazing thirst to learn, to have her brain and mind work to overcome her lost physical senses, a tutorial miracle that came three months before her seventh birthday. In her words,

> The most important day I remember in all my life is the one on which my teacher, Anne Mansfield Sullivan, came to me.... I felt approaching footsteps, I stretched out my hand as I supposed to my mother. Some one took it, and I was caught up and held close in the arms of her who had come to reveal all things to me, and, more than all things else, to love me.

Imagine, if you will, Helen's first major breakthrough under the guidance of her teacher as they walked by the Keller well-house, where someone was drawing water. Miss Sullivan took Helen's hand and put it under the spout. Helen related that magic moment.

> As the cool stream gushed over one hand she spelled into the other the word water, first slowly, then rapidly. I stood still, my whole attention fixed upon the motions of her fingers. Suddenly I felt a misty consciousness as of something forgotten—a thrill of returning thought; and somehow the mystery of language was revealed to me. I knew then that "w-a-t-e-r" meant the wonderful cool something that was

flowing over my hand. That living word awakened my soul, gave it light, hope, joy, set it free! There were barriers still, it is true, but barriers that could in time be swept away.

I left the well-house eager to learn. Everything had a name, and each name gave birth to a new thought. As we returned to the house every object which I touched seem to quiver with life. That was because I saw everything with the strange, new sight that had come to me.

Is Helen getting you to wonder about your own frames of reference, comparisons, and learning circles? Are you astonished at how difficult it was for her to acquire the use of the word "w-a-t-e-r" compared to you when you were the same age?

In her memoir, Helen might have been thinking of you when she wrote, "Children who hear acquire language without any particular effort; the words that fall from others' lips they catch on the wing, as it were, delightedly, while the little deaf child must trap them by a slow and often painful process. But whatever the process, the result is wonderful."

Have you ever heard your family or friends use the words "an irrepressible spirit"? If not, you're reading about it now.

The understanding of the word "water" opened a whole new world to Helen: "I had now the key to all languages, and I was eager to use it." She learned many more words that day, including "mother," "father," and "teacher," but what about the meaning of abstract words such as "love"? One sunny day she and Miss Sullivan were out in the garden when Helen picked some violets and gave them to her teacher, who tried to kiss her. Helen turned away, not used to being kissed by anyone but her mother, so Miss Sullivan took her hand and spelled "I love Helen" into it. "What is love?" Helen asked, catching the fragrance of violets on her teacher's hand. "Is love the sweetness of flowers?" When Miss Sullivan said no, Helen asked if love was the warmth of the sun she could feel on her skin. Again the answer was no. A day or so later, Helen was stringing beads in groups according to size and making many mistakes, which her teacher kept pointing out. Helen was focusing on her task, trying to correct herself, when "Miss Sullivan touched my forehead and spelled with decided emphasis 'Think!'" Then came the epiphany: "In a flash I knew that the word was the name of the process that was going on in my head. That was my first conscious perception of an abstract idea."

Soon Helen was introduced to "raised letters," or braille, which accelerated her learning to read. Then it was on "to the printed book. I took my 'Reader for Beginners' and hunted for the words I knew; when I found them my joy was like that of a game of hide-and-seek. Thus I began to read."

Her mind was stimulated by her constant explorations through touch and smell of gardens and woods outside her home: "the fine, resinous odor of pine needles, blended with the perfume of wild grapes ... noisy-throated frogs, katydids and crickets held in my hand ... little downy chickens and wildflowers ... meadow-violets and budding fruit trees ... the indignant snort of my pony, as we caught him in the pasture and put the bit in his mouth—ah me! How well I remember the spicy, clovery smell of his breath."

To the sightless, deaf, and mute human came the silver lining of extraordinary development of the senses of touch and smell.

Toward the end of this chapter of her memoir, Helen imparts a further insight for you to ponder: "Any teacher can take a child to the classroom, but not every teacher can make him learn. He will not work joyously unless he feels that liberty is his, whether he is busy or at rest; he must feel the flush of victory and the heart-sinking of disappointment before he takes with a will the tasks distasteful to him." Whew! It's worth noting here that even Helen Keller, a champion of women's rights, followed the patriarchal tradition of her time in using "he" as a generic pronoun to refer to persons of both sexes.

Just before her eighth birthday, Helen's mother and Miss Sullivan took her to the Perkins Institute for the Blind in Boston, where she met blind children who knew the manual alphabet, that is, the same finger-spelling method her teacher had used with her. "What joy to talk with other children in my own language!" she wrote. She returned home after several more stops in New England and later recalled that trip as "the beginning of everything. The treasures of a new, beautiful world were laid at my feet, and I took in pleasure and information at every turn. I lived myself into all things.... The barren places between my mind and the minds of others blossomed like the rose."

Has the indomitable Helen Keller gotten to you yet? If you want more of the valor, the self-reliance in the face of huge obstacles, the relentless quest that led her to be the first blind and deaf person to earn a Bachelor of Arts degree (from Radcliffe College, part of

Harvard University), and from there into a life on the national and world stage, as resourceful and fulfilled as anyone, please pick up *The Story of My Life* and savor its seventy-five pages of contagious motivation and leadership on many of the most significant injustices of the twentieth century—which, alas, continue into the twenty-first century. Can you imagine? How far do you have to stretch your imagination?

For the purpose of this present book, however, it is Helen's iron determination to overcome her dark inner world of isolation that is so compelling on the point of concentrated self-education. Listen to her account of learning to speak in the spring of 1890, at age ten:

> **The impulse to utter audible sounds had always been strong within me. I used to make noises, keeping one hand on my throat while the other hand felt the movements of my lips. I was pleased with anything that made a noise and liked to feel the cat purr and the dog bark. I also liked to keep my hand on a singer's throat, or on a piano when it was being played. Before I lost my sight and hearing, I was fast learning to talk, but after my illness it was found that I had ceased to speak because I could not hear. I used to sit in my mother's lap all day long and keep my hands on her face because it amused me to feel the motions of her lips; and I moved my lips, too, although I had forgotten what talking was.**

Miss Sullivan took Helen to see Sarah Fuller, who was principal of the Horace Mann School and had worked with Alexander

Graham Bell on methods of teaching deaf children how to speak. Helen's description of her first steps to speaking is mesmerizing.

> **Miss Fuller's method was this: she passed my hand lightly over her face, and let me feel the position of her tongue and lips when she made a sound. I was eager to imitate every motion and in an hour had learned six elements of speech: M, P, A, S, T. Miss Fuller gave me eleven lessons in all. I shall never forget the surprise and delight I felt when I uttered my first connected sentence, "It is warm." True, they were broken and stammering syllables; but they were human speech. My soul, conscious of new strength, came out of bondage, and was reaching through those broken symbols of speech to all knowledge and all faith.**

Before going to Radcliffe in 1900, Helen had read widely and deeply in the growing number of books in braille. She was able to digest and reflect on what she was reading in part because that was her nature and in part because her disabilities minimized surrounding distractions and trifles. But once at Radcliffe, "Gradually I began to find that there were disadvantages in going to college," she wrote.

> **The one I felt and still feel most is the lack of time. I used to have time to think, to reflect, my mind and I. We would sit together of an evening and listen to the inner melodies of the spirit, which one hears only in leisure moments when the**

> words of some loved poet touch a deep, sweet chord in the soul that until then had been silent. But in college there is no time to commune with one's thoughts. One goes to college to learn, it seems, not to think. When one enters the portals of learning, one leaves the dearest pleasures—solitude, books and imagination—outside with the whispering pines.

It is plain that Helen's mind was maturing rapidly. She wanted knowledge and wisdom, but she also wanted to pursue the all-important question of knowledge for what purpose. She began to identify more and more with impoverished workers, joined the Socialist Party, and supported Eugene Debs, its presidential candidate, in several campaigns. Her admirers wanted her to pursue her charitable activities as a role model and teacher for youngsters with similar disabilities, and she was fine with that, but she also fervently wanted to pursue justice for terribly exploited people everywhere. Those who wrote and filmed and recorded the story of how she surmounted the insurmountable as she fulfilled ever more of her life's possibilities highlighted this charitable dimension of her life and downplayed her commitment to justice and social action. She left the Socialist Party in 1912, saying that they were working for change too slowly, and joined the Industrial Workers of the World, a more radical group. In 1916, when an interviewer asked her about the advisability of this move, she famously said, "I have no use for semi-radicals!"

In 1920 Helen Keller was part of a hardy group of determined activists who founded the American Civil Liberties Union, also including Roger Baldwin, Jane Addams, Crystal Eastman, Jeannette Rankin, and James Weldon Johnson. They all believed that the phrase "We the People" in our Constitution means all of us. The ACLU, which celebrated its hundredth birthday in 2020, is dedicated to protecting civil rights and civil liberties for everyone.

As the years went by, Helen Keller's fame as a writer, speaker, and advocate for social justice grew and spread all over the world. She was the recipient of countless honors, including the Presidential Medal of Freedom, bestowed upon her by Lyndon B. Johnson in 1964. By the time she died in 1968, just before her eighty-eighth birthday, she had left an indelible mark on the lives of millions of people with disabilities, on the hearts of those who shared her passion for justice, and on the soul of her country.

Frames of Reference Revisited

Do take time in your own solitude to reflect on the lives of Benjamin Franklin, Frederick Douglass, and Helen Keller, who offer many striking frames of reference as you think about what their triumphs might mean for your own journey into learning, teaching, and elevating your life in coming years. Consider, for example, the important question of what motivated these three super-citizens once they had overcome their personal circumstances and entered mature adulthood. It seems that all three were driven by a desire to make the world better in their own way. They moved from a focus on their own liberation from the difficulties they faced in childhood to larger frames of reference for more leverage that led to their work for social justice. They developed formidable talents and used every human energy to persist, to create, to overcome, to motivate, and to bring out the best in people and institutions.

By now I hope you're using frames of reference in your thinking processes. They're a marvelous educational tool and a fascinating way for you to expand your intellect, control or elevate your emotions, and relate to other age groups. To begin with, if someone asks you, "What's this frame of reference stuff?" you can play a little game. "Well, do you like sunny days over cloudy days?" you ask. "I don't like gloomy cloudy days, just sunny ones," comes the reply. "Well, without cloudy days there is no rain, and without rain there is a water shortage and farmers have trouble growing our food. Are you still sure you want only sunny days?" you ask. "Wow, I didn't think of that!" You see, no frame of reference, no context.

In my family of four children—two girls and two boys—we were educated not only by our parents every day, but also by our big brother, Shaf, who loved to teach his younger sisters and brother. As noted, he introduced us to the dictionary, and then to a spanking new *Encyclopedia Americana*. Later he drew us to the more academic, exceptional *Encyclopedia of the Social Sciences*. Right there in our living room, he showed us how to use these weighty volumes, even pointing out where the *Encyclopedia Americana* went into made-up history, as with the fabricated reasons it gave for the US Marines helping to overthrow the Native Queen of Hawaii, Liliuokalani, stating that the Marines were invited there when in reality the US took the Hawaiian Islands at the behest of wealthy white planters who opposed the Native population's rights. Then the US annexed the islands in 1898. Shaf, before going back in September to his studies at the University of Toronto in Canada, would assign us specific books to read. Some were pretty heavy going for our age, but we felt so respected by him for thinking we could understand a book on philosophy or the nature of music or poetry that we upped our game.

How about you? If you have younger siblings, in addition to playing games and sports with them, have you found opportunities to show or teach them things that educate? Helpful to becoming your own best teacher is to try teaching your younger sisters and brothers and their friends. You can discover how much you love doing this if you just take the opportunity, and the little ones will delight in receiving your attention.

For example, there is a lavishly illustrated book from Spain written for your age group with the alluring title *The Alhambra Told to Children*. I can imagine you reading this colorful thirty-five-page storybook to the younger ones and inviting them to discover this world-famous "little city within the city of Granada" that was built about a thousand years ago by the Moors who then ruled Spain. The poets of Alhambra have called it "Paradise on Earth," "a ruby on the temples of the city," "a treasure of harmony and light." It attracts tourists from around the world.

Exploring the Alhambra is breathtaking. There are exquisite gardens, the Court of the Lions, the Royal Baths, the Court of the Myrtles, the Hall of the Boat, the Queen's Closet, the Hall of the Sisters, and the Stairway of the Cascades. Your younger friends will see the history surrounding these magnificent edifices as different waves of invaders conquered Spain but never damaged the Alhambra. In fact, they added to its stunning beauty and to its fascinating legends.

Reading to your younger siblings and friends is just one among many activities that you will learn from and enjoy. I'm sure you can easily think of many others, but what about your older siblings? Can you show them a thing or two about nurturing their minds? As sexually maturing young people, they're probably preoccupied by other urges, distractions, and relationships. You're a little time away from those often insecure days, which gives you a perspective they may not have anymore. Give it a try and surprise yourself!

Few teenagers can avoid temper tantrums or moodiness or unpleasant behaviors that sometimes persist for days or longer. Parents are then beside themselves wondering what to do or who can help. Instead of just watching from the sidelines, offer your parents frames of reference or broader perspectives, or do this directly with your big sisters or brothers if you've watched them become morose, surly, unhappy, and withdrawn except for occasional bursts of anger over mostly nothing. Or if they're starting to indulge in vaping, tobacco, alcohol, or street drugs, or if they're seemingly without ambition and falling behind in school. But you know they're basically good kids. Let's say one of them is your sister. Invite her to a question-and-answer game at the right time at home, maybe when she's in a good mood or being helpful or it's her birthday. Fashion the game together so your sister agrees to let you ask the questions. If you do this well, it can be a maturing experience for both of you.

Here's a suggested shake-it-up dialogue to clarify what I mean. It may seem unrealistic, I know, or perhaps impossible for you and your family, but here goes anyway.

Tween: We love you, but you seem unhappy and withdrawn.
Teen: Yup.
Tween: Can you swallow?
Teen: What? Of course.
Tween: Well, some people have great trouble swallowing their food and even drinking water. How about your vision? Can you see?
Teen: Of course.
Tween: Well, some people can't see at all and have to use a white cane and a seeing-eye dog.
Teen: So?
Tween: Can you hear?
Teen: I wish I couldn't hear *you*.
Tween: Well, some people can't hear at all and have to use sign language.
Teen: Tough.
Tween: Can you run like a deer?
Teen: Maybe not so fast.
Tween: Well, lots of people can't run or even walk very well, and they're in constant pain. And how about your fingers? Are they subtle and strong?.

Teen: Yeah, got a great grip on my tennis racket.

Tween: Well, some people with arthritis have fingers so bent they can hardly pick anything up. And is your heart strong?

Teen: As far as I know.

Tween: Well, some people have weak hearts and trouble breathing. They take medicine daily and never know when their heart is going to pop.

Teen: That's kinda scary.

Tween: How's your memory?

Teen: As good as anyone's, I guess.

Tween: Well, lots of older people have lost or are losing their memory. Some can't even recognize their own children.

Teen: So they're losers.

Tween: Can you sleep?

Teen: Like a baby.

Tween: Well, many people can't sleep much without medicine, which may have harmful side effects. They wake up every hour and walk around before they try for another hour. Hey, are those new sneakers you're wearing? How many shoes do you have?

Teen: Six pairs at least.

Tween: Millions of people in the world are lucky just to have one pair of sandals, and they often cut themselves walking or pick up fungal infections.

Teen: Yuck.

Tween: You have two parents, Mom and Dad. Some kids your age have lost their parents. They're orphans, they're

> in foster homes, or worse, they're homeless on the streets or in some stairwell. You get what I'm getting at, don't you? Is your perspective, your attitude a little more positive than it was a few minutes ago? Can you see what a good future you can build for yourself with all the advantages you have?
>
> Teen: You're an obnoxious little pest, but I guess I have to admit that you've given me something to think about and gotten me out of my funk a little.

Realistically, you may not achieve such an extensive exchange with your teenage siblings, but the point can still be made about helping them recognize what's good in their lives and what will foster the degree of self-control required of a mature mind. Youth suicides are associated with extremely narrow frames of reference and gut-wrenching emotional loneliness despite all our instant tools of communicating electronically. I've always preferred face-to-face or telephone conversations because I like to hear the voices of friends or family. A real human voice can be a lifeline.

Moving from Knowledge to Action: Developing Healthy Habits

Let's shift gears to a self-exercise that can move you from an interest in absorbing knowledge to a decision to take some action, such as changing what you eat to improve your health.

Back in the fourteenth century, when the Ming Dynasty ruled China, there was a philosopher, Wang Yangming, who offered words of wisdom for people to ponder: "To know and not to act is not to know." Once you hear these words, they're hard to forget, in part because they can be a safeguard against fooling yourself or spending too much time in virtual reality.

In actual reality, many tweens in our country have a deadly diet. If you're walking through a drugstore or a 7-Eleven past row after row given over to sugar in all kinds of colorful dyes and packages, do you stop and buy raisins or trail mix? They taste good too, but you may often go for the sugar high which leads to other diseases later on in life when your doctor sends you to the pharmacy counter. Thus, the drug store profits on both ends.

Hundreds of years ago, your ancestors didn't have such products to tempt them. They had what was locally grown by peasants, serfs, or farmers, often themselves, assuming they were free to farm. They ate their vegetables and fruits whenever they were available. They ate what their families raised or grew or picked or caught in the wild. Other than their experiences, they had no nutritional knowledge and obviously could receive no advice from nutritional scientists or dietary specialists because there were none. Still, they had a healthier diet than do millions of children today in our bountiful land—and they certainly had fewer cavities!

The big food processors and marketers want you hooked on sugar because that's more profitable than trying to sell you vegetables. Human beings evolved over thousands of years to like sweet foods. Our inherited genetics are not friendly to sugar overload, but all of us, young and old, are sitting ducks for ads urging us to buy Hostess Twinkies, donuts, breakfast cereals, soda pop, and other sugary foods and beverages. The fast-food chains also know that foods with lots of salt (fries, potato chips) and fat (hot dogs, cheeseburgers) will make your lips smack—unless you train your brain to take control of your taste buds. Clearly, many businesses are recklessly aiming to seduce you, for profit, into a life of over-eating and obesity or other damages to your body, now and later on. I'm sorry to tell you again that the percentage of youngsters who are either obese or overweight has skyrocketed since I was in school, to about 60 percent of your age group.

In 2020, Michael Jacobson published *Salt Wars: The Battle over the Biggest Killer in the American Diet*, which you and your family should read together and then move away from a high-sodium diet if you're on one.

Also enlightening is an opinion piece in the *New York Times* of January 9, 2021, "Why Your New Year's Diet Is Doomed," by Mark Bittman, who is on the faculty of the Mailman School of Public Health at Columbia University. In it, he explains the grip of ultra-processed foods containing ingredients that are "never or rarely used in kitchens," in the words of Brazilian scientist Carlos Monteiro and his colleagues. Look for Bittman's latest book, *Animal, Vegetable, Junk*, published in February 2021.

A little story from my childhood may help you figure out how you're going to defend yourself against bad food choices. One day my eight-year-old brother was sitting at our kitchen table for lunch when my mother brought in a large plate of fresh carrots, celery, and radishes. Ralph immediately made a face and declared, "I don't like them. I'm not eating them." This was a departure from our family practice of not complaining about food on the table, trusting our parents to know what was good for us and watching them eat the same food with us. However, on that day my brother put his little foot down.

My mother, Rose, having three older children, knew what to do. She leaned toward him with her inquiring smile and said, "Don't you know that these fresh vegetables will make you stronger so you can be the fastest runner in your class? You'll feel better too." Ralph was not moved. "I don't want them, I don't like them at all!" he cried out. My mother persisted. "You keep saying *I* don't like them, *I'm* not eating them. Who is *I*?"

Now my brother was confused. "What do you mean, Mother? I is me, Ralph." She replied slowly, "I don't think so." "Is *I* your heart, your liver, your kidneys, your lungs?" By this time Ralph was really puzzled, which gave my mother an opening to continue by kindly saying, "Ralph, I think I know who *I* is. *I* is your tongue. Why are you allowing your tongue to turn against your brain. Now, eat up, they're very good for you." And that was that! She left quite an impression on my brother, who tells the story of this memorable exchange to this day. And he now relishes carrots, celery, radishes, and an array of different kinds of fresh vegetables.

Mother taught us the lesson that is the secret of most food companies' advertising traps— that is, doing what they never dared to do when I was your age. Now they dare to bypass and undermine parental authority (a move you will not welcome when you have your own family) and sell directly to young children products that informed critics have called "junk food and junk drinks." They aim at the tongue, the taste buds. They want you to pour more sugar, more fats, and more salt into your body without knowing anything about what's on the product labels, such as how many empty calories you're digesting along with ingredients that make quiet, dangerous, long-term war on your body and its health.

Take the ads for Coca-Cola or Pepsi, which show healthy, active families with happy children. They open the cans with gusto and swallow with more gusto. Suppose the Tooth Fairy descended on your shoulder to say, "Hey, kiddo, what if you were making your own can of soda. You've put in the water and the secret formula for the syrup. How many teaspoons of sugar do you want to add to the mix? I'm going to count. Raise your hand when you think it's enough. One? Two? Three? Four?" By now you've probably raised your hand. Well, here's what you're getting in a can of Coke: ten teaspoons of sugar! "Wow," you might say, "I wouldn't have used that much." Also, you may want to learn how to read the labels on processed foods and drinks. Look the brand names up online for more information. Better yet, drink water. After years of expanding soda consumption, water has now overtaken soda as the drink of choice. As I've said, information works. Soda, especially in large daily quantities, is very bad for you from your teeth to your toes. Some people are finally getting that science-driven message.

When it comes to fresh fruits and vegetables, did you know that the circled organic label from the US Department of Agriculture means more than food grown without pesticides, herbicides, and other chemicals? Find out how much more the organic label excludes, such as the controversial genetic engineering of food crops.

Quite a few consumer protection groups have worked hard for the last fifty years to pressure the food companies to give us more truth and more choices. Decades ago, most of the breads sold in grocery stores were amazingly spongy brands like Tip Top and Wonder Bread, bleached of nutrients natural to wheat. My mother called them "paste." Instead she baked for us, terrific loaves of whole wheat bread.

Years later, in her memory, we launched the Rose Nader Baking Project, which reflected her passion for good nutrition as well as her belief that children should do useful work in the care of their household, including the preparation of food. She had always loved to bake bread with us and the neighborhood children, who then got to take a loaf of fresh bread home for their evening meal. She knew that baking would build their self-confidence and generate ripple effects that would improve their academic work and other pursuits. More important, it was time together to talk and for her to find out what was on our minds.

For the project, we used the ovens in the home economics department of our school. We ran the project for two consecutive years, holding classes once a week for four weeks, with a different recipe each week, starting with my mother's basic bread recipe. While the bread was baking, the students were taught how yeast worked. They learned to identify the different grains that a volunteer brought in, along with a hand mill, and then they took the milled flour home. Grandmothers volunteered to teach their grandchildren how to bake. The students made pizza and invited their family members, introducing them to the group and learning how to host. Both parents and children saw different sides of each other, and there were many touching moments.

The class could only accommodate twenty students. There were many more sign-ups than that. Though the enthusiasm of families and their children was plain to see, the project was discontinued when the school decided to use the home economics space for computers. The ovens disappeared. There was much disappointment over the lost opportunity to strengthen student self-reliance and self-confidence. Sadly, the story of the Rose Nader Baking Project is just one example of many outstanding projects for youngsters that should have been models for similar efforts all over the country but that came to an end despite rave reviews from families and children.

Becoming an Informed Consumer

Thankfully, there are far better choices available in supermarkets today than there were a few decades ago. Informed consumer demand is driving the ship toward healthier food. But—and this is the big but—you'll have to want to be informed in order to move with your mind and not with your tongue, and to realize that nutritious food is delicious food, less sugary and fatty and salty than the other items sold across the supermarket shelves. After you enter the world of nutritious foods, lots of junk food doesn't leave such a good taste in your mouth at all. Once in a while, I still enjoy a good ice cream or some salted nuts. As Dr. Michael DeBakey, a pioneer in open heart surgery and an author of bestselling books, used to say, "Everything in moderation." In other words, binging is bad, even with good food, because too many calories can make you overweight or obese.

One of the best consumer groups driving what some have called the "nutrition revolution" these past fifty years is the Center for Science in the Public Interest, headed by Michael Jacobson. With a PhD in microbiology from the Massachusetts Institute of Technology he could have taken a high-paying job with any one of the big food processing companies that needed what they called "food chemists." He thought more highly of his knowledge and skills. In 1971, along with two other scientists, Al Fritsch and Jim Sullivan, he started CSPI, which worked to get good food into school cafeterias, vending machines, and homes, encouraged home gardens, and tried to get harmful additives and junk foods and drinks off the marketplace.

Mike Jacobson, like few others, knew how to dramatize "junk food" on major national television talk shows as those hosted by Phil Donahue, Mike Douglas, and Merv Griffin.

He really shook up the big food companies with his energetic challenges and regular national food days. He attended their business conventions, jumping onto the stage to make brief but stunning criticisms of what they were doing, especially deceiving and harming children with their seductive advertisements and lavish promotions.

I can't do better than to refer you and your friends to CSPI's popular newsletter and its website, nutritionaction.com. Mike Jacobson invites you to get really excited about nutrition and health so that you know enough to teach your friends and others. Think of yourself as a budding scientist on the internet or at the dinner table. Healthy living is what's smart, not high-calorie undernourishment that clogs your mind and dangerously jams your arteries at the same time.

Youngsters need to develop willpower to oppose the sly daily temptations of the giant food marketers. They spend billions of dollars to study you and often know more about your age group than your parents do, and they use this information to entice your nose, your eyes, and even your ears on the way to turning your cravings against your brain. The next time you walk into Dunkin' Donuts or McDonald's, observe how the aromas, graphics, just about everything goes after your senses so that your mind begins to signal, "Take me, I'm yours." It gets so overwhelming that if you surrender to these sensory stimuli, your very taste buds become so conditioned that good soups, fresh fruits, and vegetables have a strange taste. Scientists have made such observations. Fast-food and processed-food companies, with their testing laboratories and their surveys of your psychology and vulnerabilities, are trying to turn you into junk-food-occupied territory, but you are definitely not too young to resist. Consider that growing numbers of your age group are deciding to become vegetarians or vegans. Maybe you're one yourself.

If your teachers are not covering this important ground

thoroughly enough—although more are doing so today than years ago—and if your cafeteria is catering to artificial tastiness because your unthinking friends are shoving aside fresh apples or oranges or carrots or spinach or mindlessly dumping them into the trash, remember to turn your back on the pack and become a leader. You have hundreds of scientists and the Food and Drug Administration and the US Department of Agriculture on your side, not to mention your school nutritionist. They just need help from informed youngsters like you—they might call you an "influencer" within your circle of friends—to straighten out classmates who are lured into scorning good food.

Again, recall that ancient Chinese philosopher and his dictum "To know and not to act is not to know." Mere knowledge can achieve little, mere knowledge can soon be forgotten, but *using* what you know is life-changing. Science writer Jean Carper's book *Food—Your Miracle Medicine* (1994) was early in many ways in conveying the importance of good food for maintaining good health. As someone once said, with little exaggeration, "You are what you eat." When you apply what you know to your own daily life, when you teach your friends what you've learned (remember Ben Franklin), it's not likely that you're going to forget what you know. Your knowledge becomes a deep part of you. It gives you a true level of self-control as you wrest your wellbeing from greedy sellers who only care about making a buck off you, like those cigarette companies that used to hand out free and deadly cigarettes to kids your age as they were leaving school. These profiteers hooked kids on a lifetime of smoking that often ended with a case of agonizing lung cancer, or other tobacco related diseases.

Smoking has been on the decline in the US for decades, but now we have JUUL Labs targeting and hooking young nonsmokers intentionally. They have created a public health crisis involving sickness and even death from e-cigarettes or vaping. Since 2018, the FDA has required the company to put labels on its products warning that their use is addictive. Still, shamefully and dangerously, the tobacco industry is recreating itself with e-cigarettes and the vape pen, sugarcoated as ploys to wean cigarette smokers off their deadly habit. But nicotine is still present in vaping and has addicted many, especially youngsters who do not smoke cigarettes. It is essential that you disregard the deceptive advertisements from vaping companies. They are exposing you to toxic chemicals that harm your heart, raise your blood pressure, scar your lungs and airways, and even lead to death. Go to the website of the Centers for Disease Control and see for yourself what this new epidemic, promoted by these "cool" companies, is doing to their innocent victims.

Fortunately, opposition is growing as more information from scientists, health workers, and regulators builds toward action. You can help among your own age group to block these profiteering predators. Turn your back on the addictive pen!

Your Own Body

Let's get personal in a different way. See if you can answer the following questions.

1. How many pints of blood are now circulating in your veins?
2. How many times does your heart beat in a normal twenty-four hour day? How many bones do you have in your body and where are most of them?
3. What does your liver do for you? Your pancreas?
4. Why do you have five toes on each of your feet and five fingers on each of your hands? What's this with fives?
5. Does it matter what color your stool or your urine is on any given day?
6. Can you describe what happens when you eat a full meal as it goes down into your stomach and gets digested?
7. You're hungry, you haven't had food for ten hours. How large is your stomach? After you eat a full meal, how large is your stomach compared to when it was empty?
8. When you take Tylenol or Aleve or an aspirin, what do these medications do to relieve your pain? What about unwelcome side effects?
9. What happens to your body when month after month you never exercise or play sports, when you just sit there watching the screens on your phone, your computer, and your television set?
10. What are calories? How does your body use them to keep

you alive? Just what is your cardiovascular system doing throughout your body right now?

These are not simple questions, but not knowing the answers might get you wondering what was so much more important in your school classes than learning about your own body.

Fortunately, you can find a lot of reliable information on solid websites from the famous Mayo Clinic in Rochester, Minnesota, from the Harvard Medical School, from the National Institutes of Health, from the Centers for Disease Control, and from Public Citizen's Health Research Group. And you can check out a free app, The Human Body, with an interactive model that will help you realize what a wonder your body is! You'll start making connections right then and there about what eating too much junk food actually does to the various organs of your body. You'll find on the internet some dynamic X-ray-type pictures to help you visualize what the verbal descriptions convey.

It would be interesting to know whether this scares you into corrective action or settles you deeper into the self-destructive mood of "So what, I don't care, it tastes great, and whatever will be will be," or in Spanish, "Que será, será!" You'll experience tension between such feelings and the need to make sound decisions about your body and health, a tension that can be described as the inner battle between instant gratification and longer-term health benefits, such as fewer colds, flus, and digestive ailments that might force you to take sick days as an adult. And the more you tell yourself right now what to do sensibly in your own interest, the less your parents and other grown-ups in your life will be badgering you.

You can start by playing a game between your mind and your bodily organs, with each major organ talking personally to your mind. Your heart, your liver, your kidneys, your lungs, and your teeth can educate you about how they work, what they do for your whole body including your brain, and how they all have to work together to keep you alive and well. These organs can tell you that if they stop working, you're either going to the hospital for a transplant or you're going to heaven. Of course, you have hundreds of other parts that interconnect with the major organs to keep this amazing swirling miracle we call the human body together and reacting to all kinds of impacts over many years.

In a stirring 2009 commencement speech at the University of Portland, Paul Hawken, businessman-ecologist, had this to say to the graduates:

> We are here because the dream of every cell is to become two cells. And dreams come true. In each of you are one quadrillion cells, 90 percent of which are not human cells. Your body is a community, and without those other microorganisms you would perish in hours. Each human cell has 400 billion molecules conducting millions of processes between trillions of atoms. The total cellular activity in one human body is staggering: one septillion actions at any one moment, a one with twenty-four zeros after it. In a millisecond, our body has undergone ten times more processes than there are stars in

the universe, which is exactly what Charles Darwin foretold when he said science would discover that each living creature was a "little universe, formed of a host of self-propagating organisms, inconceivably minute and as numerous as the stars of heaven."

In his speech, Hawken was pointing to the incredible complexity of our biological systems, but for now I'm just going to ask you to talk to your heart, which will talk back to you in no uncertain terms. Let's say you're a boy named Tommy and you're standing at a McDonald's counter with your family. "I'll have a Big Mac meal, with extra large fries," you say. "Yikes, kid," your heart says, "what are you trying to do, clog me up with fat and start killing me? By the time you finish eating that so-called meal, you'll have ingested enough calories and fat to clog a river!"

Your heart is a muscular organ situated in the center of your chest. Its primary function is to supply oxygen to your body and get rid of the carbon dioxide waste products. How? By collecting oxygen-depleted blood and pumping it back to the lungs, where it absorbs oxygen from your breathing and pumps out the carbon dioxide. Then the heart takes back the oxygen-enriched blood from your lungs and pumps it through the tissues of your entire body—without your having to lift a finger. Quite a miracle! At your age your heart is usually fresh and young, so you are unlikely to have a heart attack, but you can eat so much fat and other bad stuff that your heart will make you feel some pain or constriction. Being at the center of so many movements in your body, it can send you warnings you should heed.

Your liver is very important too. The largest organ in your body, it rests in the upper portion of your abdomen and is your body's chemical factory. It has far too many functions to describe here, but I'll mention a few. Generally, your liver produces substances to make your blood clot when you bleed. It regulates levels of chemicals in your body by breaking down harmful substances from your intestines or elsewhere and excreting them into your bile or blood as harmless by-products. It converts your digested food into proteins, fats, and carbohydrates.

There are many ways in which unmindful behavior or habits can damage your liver. If you drink too much alcohol or take too many drugs like acetaminophen (Tylenol) or eat too many fatty foods, you may develop cirrhosis of the liver, which can also be caused by infections such as viral hepatitis that are beyond your control. Your liver can signal its displeasure in many ways, some that you can feel or see, like fatigue, weakness, nausea, and loss of appetite. An unhappy liver can affect your brain function, turn your skin and the whites of your eyes yellow, and turn your urine dark. That's gross, isn't it? So if you start drinking too much beer and wine, imagine your living liver yelling, "You're torturing me! If you continue, you yourself will start falling apart in painful ways. Stop now!"

As for your kidneys, you have two of them, each with a ureter that drains urine into your bladder, which expels it when you urinate. Your kidneys filter waste products and excess sodium and water from your blood and also help to regulate your blood pressure. If your kidneys are not working properly, you better believe you'll feel the results in many areas of your body, even without the excruciating pain of kidney stones. If you have unhealthy habits like a bad diet, your kidneys will yell at you too and tell you to stop abusing them or else!

Your lungs are the largest part of your respiratory system. They look like big sponges that almost fill the chest. They take oxygen from the atmosphere in exchange for carbon dioxide from your body's tissues. In numerous ways they know how to get your attention. If you swallow food or water the wrong way, your lungs will cough them up. If you run too fast, your lungs will gasp for breath. When you have a cold or flu, your congested lungs will send you their message through coughing or shortness of breath and will sometimes keep you from sleeping well or playing sports. You can damage your lungs by running yourself down so much that you get pneumonia, or by overdosing on a drug, or by swallowing very hot liquids too often. If you really want to torture them, start smoking. There are some lung conditions you can't prevent, such as asthma or mysterious allergies, but you can inquire how to reduce air contaminants or sulfites in your food, both known causes of asthma attacks.

Obviously, the above descriptions hardly scratch the surface of what is known about these critical organs in that marvelous, complex body that belongs to you, and only to you, for the rest of your life. It's up to you how much more you want to learn about your body. There's plenty of free material on the internet, but you don't need to get too obsessed with the details unless you're truly interested, or later on if you go to medical school or nursing school.

For now, a little knowledge goes a long way toward taking care of yourself by listening to your body and respecting it. Who knows, there may one day be an app that can speak for your organs at the appropriate time when your mind grows reckless or inattentive or is just trying to show off, but let's hope you don't need such an outside alarm clock. It's much better to do things for yourself through self-discipline.

I hope by now you've become functionally astonished first by the miracle that is your body, and second by the critical need to be kind to your body, as though your mind could hear your body speaking directly to it. It's a sorry fact that great daily suffering in this world comes from too many human beings harming and injuring their own bodies in all kinds of preventable ways. For you, the key is connecting knowledge to changes in behavior through action. Otherwise, as one writer once bluntly said, "we're just sucking our thumbs." From knowledge to action is the motto for improving your young lives.

Becoming a Good Ancestor

I've spoken earlier of good ancestors and given some examples, but it's time for me to fess up and say that my generation has far to go on this score. Generally, today's adults by and large have not set a good example for you. Often they do not vote in large numbers (64 percent of eligible voters did not vote in the 2014 midterm elections that turned Congress over to extremists in the

Republican Party). Deplorably, they are making your generation and your children pay for their congressionally undeclared and therefore unconstitutional wars in Afghanistan, Iraq, Syria, Libya, and elsewhere. They are not being good ancestors. They are doing little to slow or stop the destruction wrought by man-made climate disruption, instead passing the suffering on to your generation.

Of course, there are some adults who are working overtime to reverse this planetary disaster, such as Bill McKibben of 350.org, Paul Hawken who started Project Drawdown, and Winona LaDuke of Honor the Earth. Why not connect with them? They would love to have you join them in their projects. Their websites invite you to come together with people of all ages and backgrounds to save the planet through education about ready *solutions*. They combine knowledge with action to move us away from fossil fuels (keeping oil, gas, and coal in the ground) to the renewable energy of solar and wind and more energy efficiency.

That praiseworthy title "good ancestor" will be handed to you in a few decades to fulfill with knowledge, judgment, and wisdom. Already Greta Thunberg and all the young people she has inspired are paving the way to confront climate disruption. For a few months in the fall of 2019, the energy of these young people inspired actress and activist Jane Fonda to join Friday climate actions at the US Congress. The young are pulling adults to the problem of climate disruption; they have put this issue smack in the middle of the table! Friday school strikes are increasingly intergenerational. As for other issues, you can easily connect with the now graduated Parkland students in Florida on gun control or with Black Lives Matter protesters on social justice. You also will have your own ideas about what's most important.

Becoming a Smart Voter

Let's talk about your forthcoming role as a voter. Better yet, let's aspire to the phrase "a smart voter." In the country of Costa Rica, the law encourages parents to bring their children with them to the polls so they can cast a nonbinding vote and become comfortable with the practice of democracy. Costa Rica has no standing army, unlike nearby Guatemala, Honduras, and El Salvador, where military, police, gang violence, great concentration of wealth in a few families, and deep poverty have driven millions of refugees to the United States. Costa Rica has escaped this turmoil and is a more prosperous democratic society in part because its voters were smart and elected better leaders, thus securing better lives for themselves.

With a few great exceptions, your schooling will not teach you to become a smart voter, will not mention the historic importance of third parties in our elections or obstacles facing voters or candidates. You will not learn about the concentration of power in a few hands. Students mechanically pledge allegiance to our flag with little emphasis on its last, all-important phrase, "with liberty and justice for all." The flag is taught as a symbol of military forces, battle actions, and wars. Our national anthem, "The Star-Spangled Banner," is militaristic and has prevailed over another frequently suggested anthem, "America the Beautiful." Unfortunately, neither public nor private schools are there to teach you that in American history "dissent is the mother of ascent," as the saying goes, and should be more vigorously studied in our past and encouraged among the students of today instead of being suppressed. Actually, most of our constitutional rights started with dissenters long ago. "Dissent protects democracy," states a favorite button of mine.

How many times have you wanted to say what you believe to be the truth, but you held back? How many times have you wanted to comment or disagree, but you held back? Who or what held you back and why? Although our educators give lip service to critical thinking, what they often actually mean is successful test-taking. As my sister, Laura, likes to say, "Standardized tests lead to standardized thinking." And, I should add, standardized curricula and study encourage conformity and sameness.

Becoming Alert to Propaganda

One way out of this dullness is to study the history of propaganda, the real "fake news," and learn how to spot it in today's world. The word "propaganda" originated in the early seventeenth century from the Congregation for Propagation of the Faith, a committee of Roman Catholic cardinals responsible for foreign missions and the training of missionaries. It's always good to search for the origin of words in that helpful dictionary. The *Oxford English Dictionary* defines "propaganda" this way: "The systemic dissemination of information, especially in a biased or misleading way, in order to promote a political cause or point of view." Also, "the means or media by which such ideas are disseminated."

During World War II, the Allied countries, led by the US, dismissed Germany's "information campaigns" as propaganda, which was elaborated to mean vicious lies, deliberate twisting of the realities of specific battle outcomes, and daily manipulation of German citizens' minds. Today in the US, the wide use of phrases like "post-truth," "fake news," and "alternative facts" shows us that propaganda has spread to our political and electoral arenas. Yet schoolchildren, who are exposed to propaganda as well, are not taught how to detect such "twistifications" (Thomas Jefferson's word) of facts, truths, or the dictionary meaning of words and phrases.

It can be lots of fun to dismantle paragraphs or pages of propaganda, and to do the same with television advertisements beamed directly to your age group, which the marketers believe to be "very impressionable." What does that description mean? That you're likely to believe, or at least to accept, these fast-moving, colorful advertisements, often featuring familiar cartoon figures to further exploit your trust? In Sheila Harty's noteworthy book *Hucksters in the Classroom: A Review of Industry Propaganda in School* (1979), she describes in detail the aggressive free distribution inside schools of manipulative promotional materials from the coal, nuclear, and food industries, to name a few.

At this point it is fitting to recall the wise words of Aldous Huxley, author of *Brave New World*, who wrote in 1927, "Facts do not cease to exist because they are ignored." Some facts are easy daily observations: the sun is out, it's raining, the factory is open, the store sells books, teachers and students came to class today, and so on. Other facts are not as visible: you may have indigestion, but is it from the food you ate, or is there some other fact-linked cause that explains your discomfort? There are historical facts like dates and names and events, but a great deal of historical "fact" is shaped by whoever is telling the story. Recall how the *Encyclopedia Americana* gave a version of the US acquisition of the Hawaiian Islands from the viewpoint of plantation owners, saying the US was invited in when in reality the Marines invaded the islands. There are facts about our legal system: the number of states whose constitutions have an impeachment clause, or the number of jury trials in the US courts. Then there are arrived-at facts, as when juries decide the facts of a case based on a "preponderance of the evidence." There are engineering facts, such as how much weight a certain bridge can safely bear or how many people an elevator can safely hold.

Medical and scientific facts at any given time may be revised or supplanted by new discoveries at a later time. Presently, an overwhelming number of scientists say that the world's climate is changing due to man-made emissions of greenhouse gases. A few scientists, often associated with fossil fuel companies, dispute this finding. How do you decide for yourself? That's a basic question, isn't it? Whether you're watching television ads aimed at selling you stuff, or whether you're listening to your teacher conveying "political" views, or whether you're poring over your textbooks, how do you sort out the truth, the facts, from varieties of propaganda containing biased, misleading, or outright false statements and glaring omissions? And in newspapers and magazines, what's the difference between an article reporting facts and an editorial opinion?

After some practice, you'll develop some rules of thumb to guide your conclusions. Commercial advertisements are not going to tell you the dark sides of their products (say, the harms of junk food, or the hidden side effects of medicines, or the hidden limitations behind the rosy descriptions of healthcare, credit card, and insurance services). Print and online catalogs are sent to tens of millions of consumers every year. They make for their consumer products specific claims of effectiveness, safety, durability, and respect for the environment. Watch out! Unless companies can give you proof of their claims, don't believe them. For example, high-end Hammacher Schlemmer sells an air purifier for $300 that "eliminates up to 99 percent of airborne viruses, mold, and germs," says the company. An air purifier that eliminates 99 percent of airborne viruses in the age of Covid-19? Highly unlikely. When a customer wrote Hammacher Schlemmer to ask for the name of the laboratory that tested the product and a copy of the actual test, a company executive wrote back without responding to the question.

The most important lesson here is that if sellers can't or won't back up their claims, don't believe them, don't buy their products, and tell your family and friends and others what you've discovered. For help, you can go to the honest, accurate *Consumer Reports* website (consumerreports.org), which takes no advertisements and does its own tests on products to find the facts denied you in commercial ads.

A primary rule of thumb is to ask about the source of the facts.

Does the source have a reliable reputation? Is some commercial interest group paying the source on the sly? Can you rely on someone you trust to filter out false or misleading parts of the message, maybe a relative or an influential person in your community such as a physician, lawyer, electrician, or plumber, someone who has a local reputation for accuracy? This rule applies to every kind of propaganda, but for now let's get back to political propaganda, which is everywhere and always has been.

What with lying and wild anonymous claims on the internet, a degraded political system, and the speed with which lies can reach huge audiences before being discredited, you're living in the rancid age of demonstrably false, distorted, sometimes outright slanderous statements. How do you protect yourself from being harmed by them personally or having your community or culture contaminated by them? Fortunately, you are also living in the golden age of truthful documentaries, exposé books, and articles. You can start by becoming a better consumer of political information. In class, perhaps you can do some role-playing as a voter and taxpayer in that regard. Part of being a smart voter comes from experience with what's going on with the candidates and their records, rhetoric, and contradictions, their proposed policies, their backers and paymasters, their debates, their responsiveness to people back home, and the like.

I am always amazed when every four years, given a choice of all the presidential candidates on the ballot, middle schoolers come out for the most progressive candidates and what they stand for, even if they're from a smaller third party. That happened with my brother Ralph when he ran on the Green Party ticket in the year 2000. He won many straw polls among middle school children. *Scholastic* magazine doesn't like to include third-party candidates when they send you their presidential election materials. The editor just offers up the nominees of the Republican and Democratic parties. Stimulated by their attentive children, some parents have objected to this bias.

The first duty of an eligible voter—eighteen years old and up— is to vote. If you want a better government that meets the needs of the people, you have to become an informed voter *and vote!* Unfortunately, a sizable majority of eligible Americans do not vote in off-year congressional elections. In 2018, 53 percent did not vote. In 2014, 64 percent did not vote, and as a result the Republicans took over the Congress and thus control over the appointment of our federal judges right up to the Supreme Court. Barely a majority of registered voters turned out in 2016 to choose the president, and the election was decided by the antiquated tiny Electoral College.

Astonishingly, voters who actually vote are a distinct minority of all age-qualified voters in the country. Some voters who do turn out choose largely on the basis of ads and slogans, party loyalty, personalities, prejudice, or a "throw of the rascals out" attitude that just allows new rascals to take their place. In Australia and a few other nations, voting in federal elections is a civic duty, required by law. Therefore, the turnout is 95 percent or more. Political parties don't have to spend millions of dollars begging people to come out and vote. Maybe the Australian model will become the subject of debate and consideration in our country. In the US, in some states and in some elections, voters can write in their choice if they dislike all the candidates on the ballot. One proposed reform would let them vote for a binding "none of the above."

Ask yourself what you have to know to make an informed choice that would be good for the country. You've already made progress simply by asking that question. Adults often spend more time deciding which campaign buttons, signs, and bumper stickers they want than evaluating the candidates. There are very few study groups formed by adults to determine which candidates really are on their side—compassionate, honest, truthful, studious— and which self-serving candidates are going to betray them on behalf of greedy commercial interests. Why not send the candidates some probing questionnaires? Or arrange meetings for serious exchanges with the candidates on the campaign trail, instead of just shaking hands with them? Or demand that local radio, television, and newspapers, which are full of paid political advertisements, report informatively on the candidates and hold real debates? Just think of how important these candidates are for your well-being. After all, at the level of the Senate and House of Representatives, over one hundred million voters are giving five hundred and thirty-five lawmakers the constitutional power to tax, to spend, to confirm presidential nominations, to investigate, and to shape foreign policy and military actions. Wouldn't your parents pay serious attention to neighbors who were given the power to spend twenty-three percent (as Congress does) of their income every year? Not to mention the power to make many other key decisions that directly affect your family, either fairly or unfairly? So much is at stake for everyone that "We the People" should take adequate time to study, meet, and instruct those running for our city councils, state legislatures, and Congress. This should be, as they say, a no-brainer. As the old Roman adage goes, what affects us all should be decided by all. Unfortunately, that does not happen. The powerful few decide for the many. A majority of citizens don't even know the names of the lawmakers to whom they have delegated enormous power! They could find out in a few minutes on the computer.

The time to decide to be different, and to become a stronger, smarter voter, is *now*, before you're old enough to vote. It may not surprise you to learn that many youngsters your age, given the opportunity in school or at home, are more interested in elections than they are when they become grown-ups. That's why some young and older people are pressing to give the vote to sixteen-year-olds, arguing that if they're old enough to work and drive, they're old enough to vote. I heartily agree. Plenty of good, useful guides on voting are available for you to chew on so you'll be prepared when you reach voting age. Discuss your views with members of your family sometime soon.

Civic self-confidence is not something you were born with; you need to achieve it. How? By really wanting to change something you know is wrong or unjust that affects your daily life, by plunging in to try to right the wrong.

What Happened to Physical Education in Schools?

Physical education has been declining all over the country ever since constant testing and other mandated federal and state programs began crowding your school hours. Here are some figures. Forty years ago, daily physical education (P.E.) was the norm for students from kindergarten through twelfth grade. The American Heart Association now finds that only four percent of elementary schools, seven percent of middle schools, and two percent of high schools have daily physical education class for the entire year. Twenty-two percent of schools have no physical education classes at all. Studies have shown that children who are provided physical education classes are more ready to learn in their academic work and that behavioral problems decline.

Ken Reed, policy director of the League of Fans, writes in his fascinating book *The Sports Reformers: Working to Make the World of Sports a Better Place* (2018), "It's mind-boggling that at a time when overweight and obesity levels are sky-high amongst our young people, physical education classes, recess, and intramural sports programs are declining."

P.E. results in healthier children, as Reed writes:

> **The overall health implications of the decline in physical activity in our schools are certainly scary. For example, Type 2 diabetes once was considered an adult disease. However, because more kids are overweight and obese, the incidence**

of the disease has increased dramatically in children and adolescents.

If current trends hold, diabetes is expected to afflict a third of the population [of our country] by 2050 (obesity is a prime cause of diabetes that will afflict nearly half the population by 2030 at the current rate). The expected *annual* cost of diabetes in 2034, according to a recent academic study, is *three hundred and thirty-six billion dollars.*

If you don't know how scary diabetes can be, please look up its awful impacts. Then let's say you want to do something about the absence or infrequency of physical education classes in your school. You begin by putting the facts together. Read Ken's book or other easily available arguments for P.E. Look for some friends to join with you in a visit to your teachers and your school principal. Don't be startled if they seem astonished by your maturity. You start by saying that your mission is to save lives, to improve health, to stimulate educational brain activity, and to increase the likelihood that P.E. for kids *now* will lead them to play more participatory sports later as adults. Rest assured that big-time medical and health associations, famous athletes, and all kinds of authors and reporters are on your side. They know that the more fit and healthy students are, the better they will perform academically.

Now you write a letter, full of facts and common sense, requesting a daily P.E. period for the next semester or the next school year. You send this letter to all the media and put it on the internet. Remember that Salt Lake City fifth-grade class who cleaned up a dump? Remember the great work of Children's Express? You can learn the citizen skills we've spoken about so that you can persist and get more teacher and student support, receiving more media attention on the way. This kind of experience increases your depth of civic self-confidence. If you agree with Ken Reed and still do nothing, ask yourself why?

The Beauty Business

A confidence-shattering anxiety that many preteens will be even more worried about in a few years, as teenagers, has to do with appearance and body shape. It is helpful to discuss right now the subject of who decides the standards for human beauty. Before photography and television, human beauty standards came out of local culture. Now, with the camera, the cosmetic and fashion companies are in the driver's seat. Their models, some as young as you, highlight a particular kind of good looks in millions of color photos and advertisements each year. You cannot escape these real or created pictures, though you should realize that not two percent of your class will ever come close to looking like these models.

In their unguarded moments, beauty companies admit that what they are selling is "hope." Maybe "illusions" and "delusions" are more accurate words. Either you ignore their manipulative drive to get you to buy their products, or you strive "hopefully," ceaselessly, anxiously, and expensively to get a little bit closer to the ideal portraits put before you. You buy hair gels and facial cosmetics.

Some of you go so far as to have invasive surgery on noses, chins, eyes, ears, and cheeks. It is hard to exaggerate the pain, anxiety, dread, sorrow, and self-hatred—not to mention bulimia, other eating disorders, and sometimes suicidal impulses—that come from surrendering your mind and insecurities to these narrow "beauty" frames, these hurtful seductions, all for corporate profits. These false standards accentuate the likelihood of bullying in school and nasty remarks, especially directed at girls who are harshly deemed "plain" or "ugly." Such standards can foster an enveloping self-loathing that is not your fault but is the cruelty of the so-called beauty industry, with its tens of billions of dollars' worth of annual sales in the US.

Ask yourself this question. Wouldn't it be a daily relief if beauty were not defined as skin-deep and requiring all those creams, lotions, enamels, dyes, powders, colognes, blush, eye and lip makeup, *and* the time used to put them on? Wouldn't it be wonderful if our culture were not run by the drive for commercial profits and instead recognized the deeper, more authentic beauty in good character, generous personality, health, fitness, compassion, a sense of humor, competence?

Anita Roddick, founder of the Body Shop, a worldwide chain of skin care stores, repeatedly tore into the beauty industry and its deceptive grip on women's fears and insecurities. She ridiculed it as a form of mind control over those who accept its commercial definition of beauty. Among her more trenchant comments was this one: "The idea that beauty is nothing more than a combination of features is ludicrous: it's about action, commitment, vivaciousness, courage, energy, self-esteem and compassion—all the things that women should be celebrated for. It's not passive, not a combination of high cheekbones in bee-stung lips." At one time she wrote, "I hate the beauty industry. It is a monster selling unattainable dreams. It lies. It cheats. It exploits women."

In line with Roddick's no-nonsense takedown of the many planned ways in which the industry gets into your mind so that you're afraid *not* to buy what it's selling, schoolteachers are shocked by how early girls are seized by commercial images. In the words of novelist and teacher Claire Messud, "By the time they get to my classroom, to the third grade, they're well and truly gone—they're full of Lady Gaga and Katy Perry and French manicures and cute outfits and they care how their hair looks! In the third grade! They care more about their hair or their shoes than about galaxies or caterpillars or hieroglyphics." Ms. Messud just wants you to protect yourself from the grasp of corporate profiteers and have you independently define yourself by your own standards, and by what you and your parents believe is best for you. Isn't that what families are all about?

Anita Roddick, who was honored by Queen Elizabeth II as "Dame Anita," set the example again and again in the assertion of equality between women and men. She hired women in great numbers at all levels of her company, and she out-achieved her male competitors in "the beauty business," a phrase she intensely disliked. She supported women in poor countries in assuming leadership roles in their communities. Above all, she showed that being a successful businesswoman meant something more than competing with or mimicking men in a male-dominated industry; the title of the book she published in 2005 was *Business As Unusual*. She ranged far and wide in her opposition to injustices, including the plight of the wrongfully imprisoned in the US. She sent effective assistance and nurses to rescue poor orphans dying from horrible conditions and neglect in Romania after the fall of the country's Communist regime. She was a role model for the half of the human race that over the centuries has been kept from fulfilling its potential alongside and beyond men.

Reacting to deep authentic beauty is a form of freedom, a personal liberation from the clutches of the cosmetic marketeers. People of all ages should be valued for the way they speak, relate, and care about others—far more meaningful than the length of a nose, the shape of the eyes and ears, the width of the brow. My mother always reminded us that in Arabic folk culture, to say someone is beautiful means both on the outside and on the inside, the presentation of the whole person. Such independent critical thinking is nourished by frequent media exposés revealing that too many of these price-gouging cosmetic products do not work as advertised, that they're a sham and often dangerous to your health, short-term and long-term. Some cosmetic companies make far-reaching claims, comparable to those of the drug companies, for their ever more chemically complex products.

You can't rely on the Food and Drug Administration to watch out for your cosmetic health and safety. They've never been given the authority to do that by the Congress, which has been lobbied for decades by the cosmetics and fashion industries. This is the case despite a landmark 1978 report by Congress's General Accounting Office listing 125 cosmetic chemicals that are believed to cause cancer.

More and more youngsters are refusing to use makeup, achieving their own natural look, and ignoring the deceptive use of the word "natural" by the beauty marketers. As one teenage girl said, "It just takes too much time and irritation." Not surprisingly, she was a good athlete who did not need to shell out a lot of money because of any insecurities she may have harbored. Once again, remember my mother's wonderfully helpful advice to her children: "Turn your back on the pack and be a leader."

The Two Great Pillars of our Civil Justice System

It's time to show you how you can use your fertile brain and dispel the assertions of adults that you are too young to understand anything about the two great pillars of our individual freedoms, which have been around since the founding of our country. I am referring to *the law of contracts* and *the law of torts*. Let's get right down to these two big challenges to your capacity to understand what affects you and your family every day of the year.

THE LAW OF CONTRACTS

What do you know about contracts? If you've ever clicked on "I agree," you'll have some notion that you're obligated to obey what Facebook, Instagram, Google and others call "terms and conditions." Like just everybody else, you'll never see the pages of fine print that these companies' lawyers have written to make sure they're the ones who are fully in charge, not you or any adult.

Here's what contracts—agreements between buyers and sellers in the marketplace—are all about. You've seen all those trucks on the highways full of products going here and there; they wouldn't be there without contracts. You download songs, movies; they wouldn't be there without contracts. You go to a clothing store to buy a jacket or a pair of shoes; they wouldn't be there on the shelves without a whole chain of contracts, many starting in Bangladeshi or Indonesian factories. Flying somewhere or taking a train to another city? Wouldn't happen without contracts between you and the airline or railroad, even though you never see them. Going to a doctor or dentist? They wouldn't be there without many contracts assuring them all the things they need for their daily work. Renting an apartment or buying a car or a motorcycle? No way without contracts between tenant and landlord or motorist and dealer. Do you use your cell phone? It's loaded with a cloud of contracts, from the manufacturers to the phone companies. Do you use credit or debit cards? They're awash in fine-print contracts.

Why? Because contracts declare the obligations between buyers and sellers, and if one party violates what has been promised, the other party can go to court to enforce payments or penalties, or to require that the task or job be done. Contracts mean predictable and stable expectations between sellers and buyers to get things done in life. In theory, that's the way they're supposed to work, at least!

What makes a contract? Sellers agree to give buyers something in return for payment, usually money. Without money or something of value—e.g., jewelry or hours of work instead of money—the courts say there is no binding contract. The glue that makes contracts enforceable or binding is consent—namely, the two parties agree to be bound by the exchange of valuable things, a sofa for money, or electricity for monthly payments.

The question of whether you really consented to various fine-print terms may arise if a complaint or rip-off happens during the life of your contract with a company. Will the power of the sellers and their lawyers succeed in getting the courts to assume you consented if the case ever gets that far? Most people usually give in and pay up. Because they want the product or service *now*, they don't have time for a hassle. Or folks don't want the sellers to damage their credit rating or that all-important credit score.

Given the fact that you're the first young generation to be directly bound by so many fine-print contracts, doesn't it make sense for you to learn some basics about the law of contracts and what you can do to defend yourself? Most adults don't have the determination to know and to act. We'd have a different country if they did. Again, remember that Chinese philosopher's insight, "To know and not to act is not to know." Except for test-taking, what good is all that knowledge you're absorbing if you don't relate it to your regular life and the lives of others? It's always important to keep this transition in mind. Knowledge is nourished by action and action is enabled by knowledge. As the ancient Persian philosopher Abu Hamid al-Ghazali once wrote,

"Knowledge without action is a means without an end, while action without knowledge is a crime."

CASHLESS KIDS

Corporations and their lawyers are really determined to take away your freedom of contract. They don't want you to negotiate the terms with vendors, to express freely your consent or rejection of those terms, and to have remedies when you're treated unfairly. That is, if you can ever get hold of the entire contract. They start early with you, earlier than you might think. Michelle Singletary, who writes "The Color of Money" consumer column for the *Washington Post*, published a column in April 2018 that stunned readers, including me, with this headline: "Why Does a 2-Year-Old Have a Credit Card? How to Protect Your Children from Identity Theft."

Criminals can target children by stealing their personal information, such as a Social Security number given at birth, "and then proceed to build a credit profile capable of duping lenders for years," Singletary wrote. Fine-print automated contracts from the major credit bureaus give these criminals many opportunities. Contracts envelop people of all ages in many ways from the moment they enter the credit/debit or newer types of payment markets, whether vulnerable to identity theft or not. More and more companies are moving away from even requiring your signature on the more traditional contracts, such as loans.

To control you more tightly, the credit industry tries all kinds of tricks to reduce your use of cash and checks, imposing extra charges for paying by cash, or simply saying they won't sell you goods and services paid by cash or check. Period. Some new restaurants are refusing cash from customers who walk in for a meal. Customers are rebelling, lawmakers are taking notice and protecting cash purchases, and some of these eateries have backed down.

Amazon is starting no-cash stores. For years, FedEx has refused customers who pay by cash or check. All airlines now require a credit/debit card to purchase anything on board a flight. Because cash is legal tender, the government requires such companies to tell you in advance through store signs or website notifications that they don't take cash.

Studies have shown that when you pay by credit/debit card, you are more likely to spend impulsively and be charged more, and you will definitely lose your privacy too. Vendors will sell your personal information to other vendors. And they can more easily charge you penalties, late fees, or stiff bounced check fees because they have taken control of your credit and credit card number. Buying with plastic can become a trap. Your relationship with Facebook or Instagram or Google may be free, but internet and credit card companies know what products you buy and how frequently, and then they sell this information to advertisers and other commercial interests at a large profit, which invades your personal privacy big-time. That's how Facebook makes its billions of dollars. One close observer put it this way: "When a company gives you something for free, as Facebook does, beware because you then become the *product* in ways you cannot even guess." Big online chain stores have even started to use all this data to charge buyers different prices for the same products and services.

Wells Fargo is a huge national bank. In 2016 it was caught charging its customers for millions of fake bank and credit card accounts that the customers didn't want and didn't even know about. Some of them lost their credit ratings and even had their homes foreclosed. This was a corporate crime, but Wells Fargo could not have committed it if its customers had to pay by check or cash, because the customers would've asked, "What is this for? We didn't want or consent to it." No Wells Fargo executives were even prosecuted.

With cash, you can also keep your purchases private and you are less likely to binge on your parents' credit line. When you have to pull out your wallet and actually count out cash, you are likely to become a more responsible consumer, more likely to think carefully about whether your purchase is a real need or a discretionary item or an impulsive whim. In short, cash helps you stop, look, and listen to consider your budget and your second thoughts. Most important, *you* are in control of your own money.

When businesses go the credit/debit route, they have to pay a fee to the credit/debit companies and wait for their money to arrive. So pay cash and remind retail vendors you're doing them a favor. I pay for taxis with cash, pleasing the driver, who gets to keep the full amount owed.

FINE-PRINT CONTRACTS

It helps to read contracts. If you can't see them or understand their legalese or gobbledygook, ask vendors to put them into plain language. If they refuse, as they probably will, tell them you're out of there, no sale today. There are still places in real life where you can go to retailers and pay cash. Maybe the credit/debit boys will get the message. I value my privacy and control over my money, so I use only cash.

In addition, if you get hit with stiff fees, charges, and penalties on your cell phone or credit/debit card account, ask yourself, "Did I agree to that?" Ask your mom and dad if they were ever charged thirty-five dollars for a check that bounced. If they say, "Yes, it happens from time to time," ask them, "Did you agree to that?" This exercise teaches an important point—no, consumers didn't agree to these excessive charges. They are just *presumed* to have read and agreed to the pages of fine print when they became a customer. That includes you when you click on "I agree," a form of electronic child abuse. Someday, this contract peonage will be seen as unconscionable, if not larcenous. That's why you should start poking at vendors and questioning the contractual chains wrapped around you right now. You'll learn a lot from their answers, and you may even teach them something. They rarely encounter questioning consumers. All changes start with one or two people. Why not you and your family and friends? Try it and you'll add to your self-respect and genuine civic engagement.

I'm not going to belabor all the ins and outs of fine-print

contracts and their trap doors for consumers. If you or your parents want to read more about them in plain English, go to the website faircontracts.org. There you'll see just how far profiteering companies and corporate lawyers will go to take away your right to bargain and negotiate *before* you give your informed consent. One of the worst infringements of your contract rights is what lawyers call "the unilateral modification clause," a fancy phrase for changing the fine print *while* you, the buyer, are doing business with the seller. You may have taken a vacation with your parents using past frequent flyer miles. The airlines have fine print stating that they can change unilaterally, at any time, how many frequent flyer miles you'll need to get to your destination—say, from 30,000 to 45,000 miles. Not many parents ever knew about, much less consented to, such a reduction of the value of the miles they already earned.

Here's an off-the-charts example of deception from a Facebook contract, an example called out by law professor Robert Fellmeth as "bogus parental consent." Following severe criticism for invading the privacy of tens of millions of users, some of them your age, Facebook recently revised its "terms and conditions" for children as follows: "You give us permission to use your name, profile, picture, content, and information in connection with commercial, sponsored or related content (such as a brand you like) served or enhanced by us. . . . If you are under the age of eighteen . . . you represent that at least one of your parents or legal guardians has also agreed to the terms of this section on your behalf." Oh, sure!

It is pure fiction to claim that you or anyone of your age group consented to these terms, much less that one of your parents or legal guardians agreed to them. Yet that's what Facebook and other destroyers of freedom of contract are getting away with. So far. This is serious enough that you should take some time to think about how all this intimate information about you, swirling everywhere around the world, courtesy of Facebook and similar companies, may come back to bite you again and again in your coming years at college or at work.

There's another wild overreach in vendors' fine-print contracts, which say you have waived your right to sue them if they or their products or services wrongfully injure you or make you sick. This happens a lot with defective cars, dangerous medicines, unsafe workplaces, hazardous equipment, pollutants, and unsafe hospital conditions or practices.

Government can't take away our right to trial by jury, granted in the Sixth and Seventh Amendments to the Constitution, but companies can and do try to trick or pressure you into giving up that right when you buy something from them. The cruelty of this can hit close to home even when you're a child. Every summer millions of parents take millions of children to camp in the countryside. When they arrive, they're given a fine-print contract covering all kinds of details. The camp owners frequently demand that your parents give up their right to sue in court, that they waive in advance any liability claims if you're injured or ill as a result of staff negligence or misbehavior. That provision is weirdly called a Hold Harmless Agreement. Some fair-minded judges may refuse to enforce this dictatorial demand and allow you to have your day in court.

I said earlier that contract law is one of the two great pillars of our civil justice system. Ideally, under contract law, adults can sign contracts at will with no permission needed from anyone. But the kinds of fine-print contracts I've been talking about not only take away your contract freedoms but cross over to restrict the other pillar of your freedom—your private right to use the law of torts (the law of wrongful injury) when someone recklessly or deliberately wounds you or sickens you. In her groundbreaking book *Boilerplate* (2013), Margaret Radin, emerita professor of law at the University of Michigan, concluded that such fine-print contracts are torts or wrongful injuries in and of themselves. Those summer camp contracts I mentioned strip you of your right to use the law of torts, often pushing you and your parents into private arbitration, which mostly comes out in favor of the vendors because often the arbitrators are looking for repeat business. Compulsory private arbitration closes you out of the courtroom into a secret arbitration panel often stacked in favor of the summer camp owner, the big car company, or a hospital or chemical company. Now that you know, what's to be done to escape this bondage?

WHAT THE INTERNET KNOWS ABOUT YOU AND WHAT CAN YOU DO ABOUT IT

Let's go back for a moment to those fine-print contracts you encounter on the internet. As has been amply documented in the *New York Times* and other publications, the internet knows where you live, where you go to school, what you buy, who your friends are, when you come and go, and what your interests are, all in steadily increasing personal detail. A 1998 law called the Children's Online Privacy Protection Act supposedly stops companies from assembling and selling your personal information without parental consent, but the law is widely violated. (For details see Natasha Singer's informative article "Amazon Flunks Children's Privacy, Advocacy Groups Charge" in the *New York Times* of May 9, 2019.) Shouldn't you learn how to protect yourself? You'd be surprised what you and many millions of children in your age group can do when you exercise your collective power, put your feet down, and declare, "Enough is enough!"

You have plenty of solid evidence to back you up. In September 2019, Google agreed to pay the Federal Trade Commission $170 million, a pittance given its size, for collecting children's personal information on YouTube and using it to target them with ads. In 2014, Apple was fined more than $30 million, also a pittance, after children using its apps were charged for purchases, often of "coins" used to play video games, without their parents' consent. Groups like the Campaign for a Commercial-Free Childhood have given the FTC many more examples of deceptive in-app purchases by children whose parents couldn't get refunds.

We know that many sleep-deprived youngsters take their smartphones or tablets to bed with them. Living day and night with these gizmos can have interesting effects. For example, when I was your age, we aspired to be doctors, lawyers, athletes, pilots, artists, teachers, and musicians. According to a 2019 Lego/Harris Poll survey, 29 percent of kids your age want to be YouTubers or vloggers (I'm sure you know that means "video bloggers," but it was a new one on me), while only 11 percent dream of becoming astronauts.

Think about everything you don't like about being online—the harassment, the nasty remarks, your hurt feelings, the damage to your self-esteem. That's why some of England's top doctors have urged parents to set some limits: no sleeping with the phone, no phone during meals or family get-togethers, more physical exercise outdoors playing sports or hiking. This may be a lot easier for you to take than the absolute ban on cell phones that some parents are imposing. Turning the tables, some children are upset that their parents' constant use of their own phones keeps them from paying attention to and interacting with their families.

In August 2019, Baroness Kidron of the United Kingdom went straight to Facebook headquarters in California to tell them to stop messing with kids or else. A filmmaker and a member of the House of Lords, the baroness was largely responsible for the passage of legislation in the UK barring companies from selling directly to children, abusing their personal information, and engaging in other deceptive practices. Some members of Congress agree with her and are pushing for similar legislation in the US. Perhaps some have even seen her documentary *In Real Life*, which she made after spending months with tweens and teens and watching their online activities.

You know far more than I do about what's happening in your own daily interactions with the internet. I just want you to think more about what may be happening *to* you and why you often can't let go of that device clutched in your hands and flooding your mind and stealing your time. In this regard, I highly recommend Nicholas Carr's *The Shallows: What the Internet Is Doing to Our Brains*, a finalist for the Pulitzer Prize and "a book to shake up the world," wrote Ann Patchett in her review.

THE LAW OF TORTS: PROTECTING YOU FROM WRONGDOERS

Nestled in the scenic Litchfield Hills of northwestern Connecticut stands a museum, the only one of its kind in the world: the American Museum of Tort Law. It's right down the hill from the Winchester Historical Society in Winsted, the town in which I was born and grew up. From time to time, residents will see a school bus swinging into the spacious parking lot to drop off groups of students with their social studies teachers. They have come to learn for the first time about the American history of the law of torts.

Why did our Founding Fathers think it was so important for the emerging republic to have this law of wrongful injuries? Because it's a law that can defend and protect us. An understanding of the law of torts is especially needed in today's technologically intense society. As with the basic law of contracts, the basic law of torts is not taught in our schools in a useful way, if it's even mentioned in regular classes or course work. This is the case even though the students' daily lives are affected by whether the tort law is used as envisioned by our Founding Fathers and the Constitution they drafted that hot summer in Philadelphia in 1787.

At the museum, the students and their teachers file in through the gift shop, having little idea what they are going to experience. They are greeted by Richard Newman, a tort law scholar of thirty years who tried many personal injury cases in court. He is now the museum's legal advisor. He invites the students to read the introductory words on a wall panel of the wise judge Learned Hand: "If we are to keep our democracy, there must be one commandment. Thou shalt not ration justice." Mr. Newman then guides them to a graphic timeline showing the evolution of tort law beginning in medieval England.

In those days, when people injured or killed each other, the victims had two choices. Either do nothing and suffer the injustice, or exact revenge on the perpetrators or their relatives. The people and the ruling classes began to question this disruptive way of settling scores through cycles of revenge. They conceived of an open trial in a law court where disputes between perpetrators and victims were decided by a judge before a jury of their peers. In retrospect, this system has to be seen as one of the most remarkable innovations of any civilization. As it evolved over time, it placed in the hands of twelve jurors this one responsibility for the finding of *facts* in the dispute, and left the judge to instruct the jury about the applicable law. Except for the private deliberations of the juries, all was out in the open before the community.

In the US, as the law of torts developed, the loser could appeal the trial court's decisions to a higher court. In addition, the judges' decisions began to be written down and used as a guiding precedent for future cases. More and more cases built up a body of law and legal practices that made for both stability and a gradual change in society as its economies, its technologies, and its values about right and wrong evolved as well. All this was called the *common law of torts*, which enlarged the rights of the injured people (the plaintiffs) on a case-by-case basis. There was to be minimal interference by legislators who were likely to be influenced by wealthy interests not known to be committed to equal justice under the law.

Richard Newman guides visitors through the exhibits and the vibrant graphics that show cases involving factory machine defects, poorly secured apartment building doors, unsafe cars, carcinogenic asbestos in the workplace, deadly tobacco marketing, dangerous toys and much more. (You can now take a virtual tour from wherever you are—see tortmuseum.org.) He explains the multiple purposes of tort law verdicts and settlements: (1) *compensation* for the victims' economic losses, pain, and suffering; (2) *public disclosure* of hazardous products, services, and conditions to alert citizens and sometimes to show the need for basic government required safety and health standards; (3) *deterrence* of similar dangers that might be exhibited by other companies, parties, or individuals; and (4) *punishment* through additional punitive damages for very serious crimes and gross recklessness.

When visitors ask Mr. Newman how plaintiffs can afford to pay for lawyers who charge hundreds of dollars an hour, he describes the *contingency fee system* special to tort lawyers. The plaintiff hires an attorney who will charge only a percentage of any verdict or settlement won but will not demand payment if the plaintiff loses. The contingency fee, unique to this country, has been described as "the key to the courtroom door" for the vast majority of wrongfully injured persons unable to afford lawyers to bring the case. In the words of Georgetown University law professor Joseph A. Page, who carefully selected the cases for the Tort Museum, the contingency fee "helps promote equal justice for all citizens." Of course, well-heeled defendant corporations, with their legions of lawyers, can often win a jury verdict and receive public exoneration, as can other defendants. Overall, however, given the millions of wrongfully injured persons every year, tort law is not used much. Only a tiny percentage of victims connect with a lawyer, perhaps partly because they fear the pressures of a lawsuit and a possible stressful trial. More likely, they were never taught, from middle school to college, the rights that this legal system of justice gives them to protect and defend themselves.

It's strange that more than a few people feel there is something disreputable or seedy about suing, even when someone or some company hurts or cheats them. I know an elderly woman whose physician perforated her colon when she went in for a colonoscopy. She was in great discomfort and pain, and required major surgery before she recovered. Her doctor admitted it was his fault and apologized. Although a medical malpractice lawsuit in this case would have been a slam-dunk and would have been settled out of court quite promptly by the insurance company, she declined to file. Urged by a friend to consider that a lawsuit would make the doctor more careful with future patients, she still declined.

I don't think you'd want to live in a country where you were prohibited from suing a wrongdoer, particularly one who is influential or powerful. We have names for such countries. They are called dictatorships or authoritarian regimes.

In the US, suing for a just cause should be as American as motherhood and apple pie. Americans are known as people who don't like to be pushed around. Well, tort law—handed down to us by judges in control of the courts from the time of the American Revolution—is your pushback instrument. Don't hesitate to use it if wrongful injury should arise.

Taboos and the Classroom

At this point you might want to ask yourself why you aren't given the opportunity, in school, to learn about the law of contracts and the law of torts. It's not as if they don't connect with your life now. It's not as if you can't understand the basics of these two pillars of freedom in a democratic society, which give you ways to defend yourself against harms ranging from fraud, bullying, and street assaults to hazardous products and toxic pollution. Of course you can understand them, as you have just demonstrated by grasping the contents of these few pages.

I think the real explanation is that schools are reluctant to teach you about tools of empowerment that so often involve the misdeeds of the business community. Companies can and do pressure school boards and elected officials to eliminate or dilute classes that teach about such wrongdoing. That's why consumer education courses in some high schools, if they are taught at all, are often taught at a general level without mentioning specific companies and their brand-name products. A recent book by Richard Panchyk, *Power to the People! A Young People's Guide to Fighting for Our Rights as Citizens and Consumers* (2021), will fill such gaps in your course work with fascinating detail.

As you might expect, tools for justice can hardly be discussed in class without mentioning the injustice they're meant to prevent or penalize. In past centuries, women who fought for the right to vote argued against the male-dominated culture by pointing to the injustices arising out of their *not* having the right to vote. African Americans, Native Americans, and other minorities who organized for equality and justice pointed to the vast cruelties of slavery, segregation, genocide, domination, displacement and bigotry. Such indictments are too unsettling for many educators. They want to avoid controversy and pressure from people in power who think the truth about our history will subvert your innocent little minds.

Balderdash! (Or as you might say, "Crap!" But isn't "balderdash" an interesting word? If you want to know where it came from, look it up. The answer involves liquor.) This kind of cowardice on the part of educators is a form of miseducation, of denying students important knowledge about excessive power that keeps people passively absorbing their abuses—as it did with coal barons who operated dangerous mines for decades in West Virginia, Kentucky, and Pennsylvania with little or no redress for the miners killed in predictable and preventable "accidents." Both public and private schools long ago accepted their submerged, submissive role in such matters. The all-important matter of *power* in society—who has it, who doesn't have it, who should have it, how the rule of law should restrain, discipline, or prevent its excesses and its inequalities—well, you get why schools turn the other cheek. Brian Schultz's *Teaching in the Cracks*, mentioned earlier, is aimed at helping teachers face this challenge.

Your and your parents shouldn't turn the other cheek. A factual understanding of how economic, political, technological, and cultural power affects the basic values of freedom, justice, equality, health, safety, responsibility, and accountability is crucial to present and future generations, and crucial to a working democracy. This understanding sits at the very core of what it means to be an engaged citizen in a democracy! We must not be a nation of technically trained or underemployed serfs if we are to survive and prevent the real oncoming perils of the future in our country and the world.

Smoking: A Case Study in Confronting Power

When I was your age, people were smoking in places that today would astound and irritate you to no end. People smoked in airplanes, buses, trains, and taxis. They smoked in hospital waiting rooms, schools, restaurants, supermarkets, sports arenas, restrooms, factories, and offices. Many doctors smoked like chimneys. Television anchors like the great Edward R. Murrow of CBS smoked right on air while he was delivering the news! That certainly doesn't happen today. Let's look at how much and by whom progress has been made.

In the bad old days, smokers would blow smoke into nonsmokers' faces and then ask them why they weren't smoking. Nonsmokers, often with children in hand, meekly took this assault on their health year after year. Such was the power of the big tobacco companies like Philip Morris and R. J. Reynolds, all the way to their giving free cigarettes to youngsters walking out of school, as I've already noted. Their studies showed that hooking kids early kept them addicted and buying cigarettes for an often shortened lifetime.

Then, in 1964, something historic finally occurred. The US Surgeon General, Dr. Luther Terry, delivered an overdue report linking cigarette smoking to lung cancer and other diseases. The Surgeon General's Reports on Smoking and Health began to come out annually and document the deadly effects of tobacco—over 400,000 deaths a year in our country. In the 1950s, almost 50 percent of adults in the US smoked at least a pack a day. Now that figure is down to about 15 percent. Real progress!

What happened in the intervening years? Doctors, lawyers, and millions of nonsmokers, including the parents of asthmatic children, all started to object. Doctors warned their patients. Lawyers began suing and getting inside information from the tobacco companies, which led to even more damaging information. Tobacco company insider whistleblowers got on major national television shows such as CBS's *60 Minutes*. Nonsmokers started to speak up, demanding to know why they had to breathe air polluted by the exhalations of smokers. Citizen health groups were formed for action. Flight attendants stepped forward to speak of being burned by careless smokers as they walked down the aisles, and of the mess they had to clean up after coughing spasms by smoking passengers. Michael Pertschuk, the persuasive chief counsel for the Senate Commerce Committee from 1965 to 1976, roused members of Congress to take on the tobacco lobby.

Cigarette ads on television and radio were dropped by the industry after the Federal Communications Commission ruled that the stations had to carry anti-cigarette ads. By the early 1980s, no-smoking sections were required on all airplanes, trains, and buses. Later, smoking was banned entirely on mass transit, and all kinds of businesses and public places enforced no-smoking rules in hotels, apartment buildings, and even bars. The result is what you now see—a few smokers huddling outside buildings taking a few drags before they go inside to work, shop, or catch a movie. High sales taxes on packs of cigarettes helped reduce consumption, especially among younger smokers.

Michael Pertschuk, a pioneer in the anti-cigarette drive, estimated that at the peak of this drive in the 1980s, there were no more than a thousand individuals in our country working full-time toward a tobacco-free society. They labored in various professional, media, and civic capacities, but they had a huge number of Americans rooting for them. The all-important factor of public sentiment, or public opinion, was behind them.

This campaign is a sparkling illustration of *speaking truth to power*. Through factually informed citizen action, the once mighty tobacco industry, with its control over elected officials and the mass media, was stripped of its addictive hold on our society. Stubbornly, the tobacco/nicotine industry has come back with its Plan B, the vaping epidemic, trying to hook—yes, you guessed it—young people who are not smokers.

A number of youth initiatives are pushing back against this deadly teenage addiction so youngsters don't become addicts in their adult years. The Campaign for Tobacco-Free Kids aims at this important goal. The voices of youth are critical and powerful in persuading their peers and elected officials to fight against a venal but declining tobacco industry and its deceptive marketing and powerful propaganda.

The Campaign for Tobacco-Free Kids sponsors the Take Down Tobacco National Day of Action, a global rally for the first tobacco-free generation. The group informs us that "youth tobacco rates are at a 20-year high in the US due to the worsening youth e-cigarette epidemic, and tobacco is still a leading cause of death in the US and across the globe." You and your friends can easily get involved in this essential work. See tobaccofreekids.org to learn all about their programs and resources, which you might want to tap for a school project.

Challenging today's power must not be a taboo while you're learning in school how our forebears took on powerful wrongdoers to make America better. I find it interesting that kids your age are encouraged to become engrossed in fictional tales of power where the evildoers threaten the good guys. The *Star Wars* and *Harry Potter* movies and books are vivid examples of violent struggles between good and evil promoted to you with no attention to our real past and present life. As a result, generations of children grow up knowing vastly more about fictional power dramas in these morality tales than about real-life abuses of power affecting them, their families, neighborhoods, regions, country, and world, along with the daily hazards they may face in or on the way to school. To give credit where credit is due, it's true that the *Harry Potter* books in particular have lured millions of kids away from their screens to do some serious reading. Still, being ever more absorbed in make-believe does not prepare youngsters to become adult citizens regularly engaged with the serious conditions so many people suffer from and shouldn't tolerate.

Citizen Action/Community Action: What Is It?

There are many citizens and citizen groups who take care of us daily even if we don't know their names. Real estate agents used to have a motto for their work around the country: "Underneath all is the land." Well, underneath all democracies and their achievements are active citizens or active citizen groups or a strong citizen community or neighborhood. It's hard to point to anything we like about our country that didn't start with one or two citizens whose actions attracted additional active people who then built an active community. This has often led to changes adopted by elected lawmakers that result in a safer, fairer marketplace, workplace, or school.

There was a time when children your age could be put to work in dungeon-like factories or other dangerous workplaces, with no chance to attend school and receive an education. Then one citizen, then more, then a community movement persuaded local governments to establish public schools. Other citizen efforts got laws passed to abolish such child labor.

Building the country's early roads and bridges and parks and drinking water systems and sewage systems required this spirit of attention from citizens who took their desires and demands to local, state, and national government institutions. Your cars are safer, your food is safer, and your air and water are cleaner than they were because many years ago a few children like you grew up and organized citizen movements to make their laws and governments do these things. Most times it takes very few people to make great improvements in the lives of us all as long as the majority of us think well of what they're calling for. That's what public opinion polls are supposed to be telling us. Think of what pleases you about the communities around you—parks, libraries, public swimming pools, the local playhouse, public playgrounds, zoos, museums, health clinics, and so on. Chances are great that they started with one farseeing citizen who was then joined by more until they became a civic movement or civic community on the way to reaching a desired goal.

That's just what happened when our hundred-year-old Winsted Memorial Hospital closed down in 1996. Residents were already up in arms but not sufficiently mobilized. Our area of over 30,000 people had to have health services, especially in emergency situations when time can mean the difference between life and death. I knew we had to fight for a people-centered health facility. I and our community lawyer, Charlene LaVoie, with the help of many concerned citizens, circulated a petition to present to the governor of Connecticut. Twelve thousand people signed it in just ten days. We had the marvelous, informed aid of Fred Hyde, MD, who helped us navigate successfully the turbulent waters of healthcare in a semi-rural area. That level of civic engagement led to the creation of the Winsted Health Center. It's a motivating story recounted in a small book called *Code Blue* by Janet Reynolds, a reporter for the *Litchfield County Times*, who received a prize for her reportage.

In the 1960s, my imaginative brother Shaf was worried about what was happening to our hometown, where the factories were closing down and moving to cheaper labor in the South or being gobbled up by big companies. Empty factory after empty factory stood as a visual reminder of this serious problem. Because Shaf read widely and believed in continuing education and job training, he envisioned the creation of a community college in town. The location would be at the Gilbert High School building that had been vacated in favor of a newly constructed high school on the other side of town. When he first proposed in 1964 that little Winsted (population 10,000) should have a community college to educate and train people in the area, locals laughed at his idea. Why, no such college would ever open up in a small run-down town with rows of empty factories!

Shaf gathered about six serious believers living in our town and nearby. Because he worked seven days a week in our family restaurant, he had to meet with them there around midnight after the restaurant closed to the public. Joe O'Brien, the renowned *Hartford Courant* reporter, called them "the window tappers' club" because they tapped on the window as they arrived. Once inside, they had coffee and snacks while moving their dream forward. And move it did—Northwestern Connecticut Community College (NCCC) opened in the fall of 1965 and became the first accredited institution to enter Connecticut's newly established community college system that same year. NCCC thrives to this day and is rated one of the best community colleges in the country. Citizen action and community organization started it all, against difficult odds, step by step. The story of how a small number of citizens established the NCCC is told by noted anthropologist Dimitra Doukas in her book—*Democratizing America: Shaf Nader and the Founding of the Impossible College* (Interlink Books, 2017).

In 1993, it became clear that the old playground of my youth, simply a swing and a slide, was no longer sufficient. Little kids in Winsted needed a safe place to play, to exercise their bodies and enliven their minds. Our family proposed to undertake a community-built playscape under the direction of architects specializing in such structures. After they told us what it would cost, our family community trust provided half the money, and the other half was matched by the community itself. The children collected pennies, and when they dumped gallons of them onto the floor of the school gymnasium to take the count, the amount was a stunning $5,000. What triumph they felt! It took just one long weekend to build the structure and complete the playscape. All the skilled people we needed came from all over town with their tools—volunteer carpenters, plumbers, and landscapers. Whatever help was required was provided free. That, you see, is what citizen action, bringing out the best in people and leading to community cooperation, gets done all over the country, including your own city, town, or village. It's never enough, but it's enough for you to notice.

There is always much more to do, not just to repair and restore, but to expand the possibilities of making life fairer and better for all of us. This requires fair-minded citizens to stand up and join together to get a job done. Your street or neighborhood may have such people. When you hear your parents complain about bad businesses, politicians, and government agencies, ask them whether more informed citizen activism and community engagement would help. When people get involved in community projects with their neighbors, they discover deep enjoyment in their cooperative achievements. People around the country are starting more food co-operatives these days, organizations where the consumers or the shoppers themselves own and direct their own food market, acting as an extended family providing for itself.

My mother always believed in people getting out of their homes and connecting with their neighbors to help a charity or to improve the neighborhood or to get more people attending town meetings and voting. She was frequently seen with petitions, knocking on doors and engaging her fellow Winstedites about ways to improve the community and help the vulnerable. Sometimes people would ask her, "Mrs. Nader, you're busy raising four children and helping out in the family restaurant, so why are you spending your time working with the community?" Her answer was simple: "Because I don't see much difference between family and community. Doesn't one affect the other for better or worse?" You can fill in a lot of blanks thinking about this observation in your own neighborhood.

In the early days of the twentieth century, individual citizen philanthropists in Winsted built the local hospital, memorial library, and high school. When we know the history of how our neighborhoods and communities were built, step by step, one citizen or two or three at a time, it gives us motivation and hope for the future. This is one example of the uses of history, the importance of which history teachers like to highlight.

My mother noticed that many residents of our hometown didn't know much about its factories, schools, water purification system, or the services our stately town hall had to offer for their taxes. Winstedites often visited Highland Lake, the stores, the bars, the post office, and the library, but many fascinating places, including natural attractions and the Winchester Historical Society, were rarely visited. This prompted my mother to write an article for the *Hartford Courant* with the alluring title "How to Tour Your Own Home Town." Take a look at your town and make a list of places you might like to "tour." You shouldn't always have to go away to be a tourist.

It's often said that bad news travels fast and dominates people's attention. As an antidote, look for the good news that may be all around you. What are people you know doing to improve your community's life? Why don't they receive more visibility in the media? What can you learn from them that will spark your own initiatives?

Remember Greta Thunberg, who began to focus her attention on climate disruptions at age nine, and think about the protests she inspired to focus the attention of those in powerful positions on acting to reverse these dire trends. As noted earlier, her Friday school strikes before the Swedish parliament building have spread around the world. She, Felix Finkbeiner, and other youngsters put valuable forces in motion for climate health!

The Discipline of Discovery

Have I convinced you by now that you're your own best teacher? (My father added to this kernel of wisdom by telling us, "Your best teacher is your last mistake.") Just think about the advantages that come from a self-aware, probing, reflective mind. Almost by definition, such a mind rids itself of boredom, harmful peer pressure, and endless internet distractions, replacing these ankle weights with the joyful and invigorating discipline of discovery. Eureka! You have discovered the life of the mind, an excitement that will lead you to greater self-reliance and healthier self-care, nourished by the essential sense of self-respect.

At this point I want to give you some pertinent words from Alfred North Whitehead in his essay "The Rhythmic Claims of Freedom and Discipline."

> **What I am anxious to impress on you is that though knowledge is one chief aim of intellectual education, there is another ingredient, vaguer but greater, and more dominating in its importance. The ancients called it "wisdom." You cannot be wise without some basis of knowledge, but you may easily acquire knowledge and remain bare of wisdom....**
>
> **The only avenue towards wisdom is by freedom in the presence of knowledge. But the only avenue towards knowledge is by discipline in the acquirement of ordered fact.**

That's a mindful, isn't it? But it's worth rereading and digesting and considering from time to time. This kind of self-repetition works, especially if your teachers are trying to cram too many facts into your brain. They need to give your mind time, both to reflect on the facts and to test their validity. That's how you acquire wisdom, followed by its essential partner, judgment.

A great number of thoughtful older students and university graduates surely would have liked to read Whitehead's words when they were your age. But too many of their courses, like yours, consisted only of training, with too little time given calmly, even routinely, to nourishing the freedom to reflect. That's not likely to change in most schools anytime soon, so you have to make it happen on your own through self-education.

As a high school, college, and graduate student, I would often put a helpful quotation, saying, or proverb on my desk or my calendar to keep me alert to its meaning as I studied along. For example (another quotation from Whitehead), "Get your knowledge quickly and then use it. If you can use it you will retain it." When working on something difficult, you don't want to let your mind freeze; wise words can keep it moving.

If you've stayed with me until now, you may be wondering why I haven't spent more time discussing how to read, write, and speak more proficiently. It's because I believe that mastering these skills rests on how many enabling experiences you have on which you can draw and thrive—in other words, on self-education. Many of our greatest thinkers and writers were self-taught, Shakespeare being among the most prominent of them in Europe.

One of my schoolteachers was all about memorizing the rules of grammar: how to use prepositions, adverbs, and adjectives correctly, as well as subordinate clauses, the subjunctive mood, and punctuation marks, and when to start a new paragraph, and *never* to split an infinitive. These rules are useful, and you can earn a high grade from your teacher if you simply memorize them and their sterile examples, but you won't have learned any writing skills to speak of. I've always enjoyed expressing myself in letters to family and friends. Writing skills can be honed by writing more, especially if you write about subjects that stir your enthusiasm and your mind and are really important to you. That's been my experience in improving my writing, along with reading well-written prose.

It's helpful to have a copy of *The Elements of Style* by William Strunk, who taught English at Cornell University from 1891 to 1937. He wrote it to help his students become excellent writers. One of them was E. B. White, who went on to become a well-known *New Yorker* writer and the author of *Charlotte's Web*, among many other works. In 1959, White introduced his professor to a whole new audience with a fully revised and updated edition of *The Elements of Style*, widely known thereafter as "Strunk & White." Professor Strunk was a man of few words, often reminding his students when correcting and grading their papers to "get the little book."

Reading, writing, and speaking come from the same brain but tap into different personalities. Thus, being shy is fine for writing, but to speak before an audience you'll need to be more extroverted. Emily Dickinson, a superb self-taught poet of the nineteenth century, was an extremely private person who never gave a public speech or presentation. But what a brilliant poet she was, nurturing her creativity from a life of solitude and writing prolifically in a male-dominated society that advised women writers to keep their work to themselves. It wasn't until she passed away that her younger sister, Lavinia, discovered Emily's trove of poems and proceeded to get them published. Her poems have won her an adoring audience all over the world and are well worth your time.

The story of Emily Dickinson teaches us that a disciplined mind can accentuate the positive features of one's personality and intellect. Similarly, a moral passion for justice can be so strong that it marshals in its holder all the requisite skills leading to a wider audience for the cause. One of the greatest examples of this moral triumph of mental discipline is Frederick Douglass, escaped former slave and eloquent abolitionist. In my experience over the years, I have found that the most active citizens, those who organize the rest of us locally or at the national level, often have in common this quality of mental discipline.

A Side Note on Proverbs

I mentioned just above that I often kept a quotation or proverb nearby while I was studying, and that got me thinking about proverbs. Do you know any by memory? If you know a few of the famous ones, but just a few, join the crowd. Since the invention of the printing press in around 1440, each new generation has learned and retained fewer and fewer proverbs. Why is that? Because proverbs are part of the oral tradition, which was the main way people communicated with one another thousands of years ago. There were early but limited forms of writing—hieroglyphics and cuneiform inscribed on stone and papyrus—but if you wanted to be heard, you had to raise your voice in speech or song, and if your hearers wanted to hold on to something you said, they had to memorize it. Again, please remember the words of the Arab philosopher Abu Hamid al-Ghazali. "Knowledge without action is a means without an end, while action without knowledge is a crime," he said, a proverb passed down through the oral tradition of his people.

After books, newspapers, and other printed materials became widespread, family elders didn't have to rely as much on memory to transmit proverbs, stories, experiences, recipes, notices of gatherings, and the like. My grandparents knew hundreds of proverbs that they used regularly when the occasion demanded. My aunt Adma peppered her conversations with an amazing variety of proverbs, often with humorous vitality, that she'd stored in her mind since she was a child. It was a treat to listen to her, and it kept us on our tippy toes. When we misbehaved on occasion, our mother and father would admonish or advise us with an apt Arabic proverb. Today this might be considered cool in comparison with parents who verbally discipline their children with a loud "Stop it!" or "You'll be sorry!" or "Shut up!"

The thing about proverbs and aphorisms is that they have met the rigorous test of time, often going back centuries. They are concise and hardy nuggets of accepted wisdom that hold a folk society, its clans, and its families to common values and standards of behavior and respect. Here are some examples from my childhood days in Connecticut, translated from the Arabic. A few may sound quaint, but remember that they date from a time long before telegraphs, phones, cars, computers, and mechanization.

> —If a child was delaying a chore, there was "Wait, o mule, until the grass grows up."
> —If a child was showing off, "The more you go over the top, the more you subtract from what you're intending."
> —If a child was talking too much, "You have two ears and one mouth, so listen at least twice as much as you talk."
> —If a child was not showing respect for an elder sister or brother, "A day older is a year wiser."

The force of a proverb actually worked to straighten us out most times. I recall that it would stop me in my tracks because it gave me something to think about. The pithy message wasn't easy to ignore.

The English language is also rich in proverbs, but they are

used less and less with each succeeding generation. "A stitch in time saves nine" is easily among the top ten sayings in American history, but who says it anymore? Some sayings can be seen as contradictory—"He who hesitates is lost" and "Look before you leap," for example—but maybe not, because different situations call for the use of one or the other.

Benjamin Franklin absorbed proverbs to educate himself. Then he produced his own sayings, which have since become rooted in our culture. As I noted earlier, his short phrases and sentences filled a little book that became one of the all-time worldwide bestsellers.

You may have heard these proverbs.

- **"Absence makes the heart grow fonder."**
- **"A bully is always a coward."**
- **"Actions speak louder than words."**

Here's one observation, certainly pertinent today, that bears repeating, from the British writer Aldous Huxley.

- **"Facts do not cease to exist because they are ignored."**

One reason I like to know and use proverbs and wise sayings is that a few words can convey a lot of meaning in various situations in which you find yourself. Try them and see what you stimulate in conversations with your family and friends. I'll close here with a favorite ancient Chinese proverb that will remind you of John Dewey's "Learn by doing."

—"I hear and I forget. I see and I remember. I do and I understand."

Holidays: What We Celebrate

When official national holidays come around—Memorial Day, Fourth of July, Labor Day, etc.—you and your parents usually have the day off from school and work. Your family might plan something special for the day, perhaps a tour of your town, an outing to the park or the beach, a hike, eating out, or taking in a parade. Or perhaps you'll go to special holiday sales that stores heavily advertise.

You may wonder why these days were chosen for celebrations. Certainly not for store or online sales specials. On Memorial Day we remember our soldiers who died in wars and ponder how these wars started and whether they could have been prevented. The Fourth of July, 1776, is when our country's founders issued the Declaration of Independence from the despotic rule of King George III (see the back of a two-dollar bill for an etching of their gathering). One year in Winsted, we had young students and adults each read a section of the historical Declaration to its conclusion. We taped the reading and played it on the local cable public access station on July Fourth. The participants and their families got to see themselves in this marvelous event. Recently the American Museum of Tort Law in Winsted celebrated with a rendition of Frederick Douglass's speech of 1852, "What to the Slave is the

Fourth of July?" Eloquently and forcefully, Douglass pointed out that slaves had no reason to celebrate the nation's independence.

Labor Day falls on the first Monday in September. This increasingly neglected holiday honors the working men and women of our country who built it and keep it running every day. Labor Day is a good time to think about the state of working people, their opportunities, their pay, their pensions, their workplace safety, their wonderful skills, and why you don't see, hear, or read much about them. Columbus Day in October is in some places being replaced by Indigenous People's Day. Since 1983, the third Monday of January has been recognized as Martin Luther King Day, a federal holiday. And since 2001, March 31st has been recognized as a state holiday in California celebrating Cesar Chavez, union leader and labor organizer of farmworkers. Many volunteers are still working to make it a federal holiday. Maybe we need a special Citizen Action Day so people can discover and engage with civic America.

There are other unofficial holidays recognized by people to whom they relate, for example, Thank A Mail Carrier Day (February 4), National Collect Rocks Day (September 16), which encourages you to examine what Earth is made of right around you and possibly stumble on a real rock that is millions of years old, and World Hello Day (November 21) to encourage people to write letters to world leaders urging them to seek peace through dialogue and diplomacy.

What simple holidays would you like to create to get people to do some things they would ordinarily not have done, spicing up daily life a bit? Noticing something you would like to celebrate with others is one small way to build community and find like-minded others.

"War Is a Racket"

Wars, with their devastating weapons, are the most powerful expressions of material power. When our wars are constitutional and waged for self-defense, the resultant killing of combatants is deemed legal. When our wars are not constitutional and not for self-defense, as has often been the case in recent years, the killing is deemed illegal; it is murder. Over a million innocent Iraqis died as a result of the illegal invasion of their country by President George W. Bush and Vice President Dick Cheney. Let's not glorify war. Soldiers who have experienced the butchery and savage destruction of war do not glorify it (see veteransforpeace.org). People who have not gone to war are more likely to glorify it.

In the second decade of the twentieth century, Marine Major General Smedley Butler won the Congressional Medal of Honor *twice*. Later he wrote a widely read book, *War Is a Racket*, in which he divulged with anger and regret how he plundered Cuba for the New York banks, ravaged East Asia for the oil companies, and generally fought in defenseless countries to protect corporate profits. At the end of this little book, he published pictures of dead and dying soldiers to rip the "glory" out of war. He showed that these Americans had died and slaughtered for corporate bosses comfortably ensconced in skyscrapers with their greed.

General George Patton, a leading army commander during World War II and a famously tough guy, was once asked to define battlefield courage. His reply: "Courage is fear holding on a minute longer." When our soldiers come home, their superiors expect them to shut up about what they did and saw overseas. When some of them get together to tell the public the truth in what are called "winter soldier" meetings (a play on Thomas Paine's reference to "summertime soldiers" who deserted during the American Revolution), the corporate media does not cover their gripping stories. These soldiers don't buy into the repression of free speech by civilians once they're home. The minute a president sends soldiers to fight, kill, and die in illegal wars, they become by definition participants in war crimes under international law. I've heard that soldiers dislike politicians and others who try to shut up antiwar Americans with the curt demand to "Support our troops." The vast majority of our soldiers saw no mission or reason to invade and occupy Iraq in 2003. An independent poll in 2005 showed that over 70 percent of American soldiers in Iraq wanted the US to get out of that devastated country.

We are embroiled in endless wars in Iraq, Afghanistan, Yemen, Somalia, Libya, and other arenas, wars that were not declared by Congress as required by the Constitution in Article I, Section 8. Soldiers know these wars are tremendously expensive quagmires that generate more hatred of us from the inhabitants whose country is being destroyed. They want us out of their backyard. Some want revenge.

There are children who were your age when Iraq was invaded

and who are now soldiers in Iraq and other countries. Trillions of dollars wasted in blowing up these countries and their people could have been used to repair our crumbling schools, highways, bridges, public transit, parks, drinking water systems, and other public works. Shouldn't you be able to have factual discussions of these situations, and of the politicians who made these illegal decisions about wars, in your history, government, civics, or other social studies courses? That's what historian and World War II veteran Howard Zinn asked himself as he wrote *A People's History of the United States*, first published in 1980. (Years later, this popular book was adapted for youngsters as *A Young People's History of the United States*.) If your teachers aren't allowed to use such history books, you'll probably have to educate yourself, and all the better if you read one of these books with your family and friends. It's what I referred to earlier as big talk replacing some of that daily small talk. Big talk nourishes an informed people who won't be lied to or flattered by a tiny group of imperial plutocrats and autocrats who wave the flag in your face and sugarcoat historical realities.

As you probably know, we have military academies in our country: West Point, the Naval Academy, the Air Force Academy, and others. Where are the Peace Academies to prepare young peace advocates for professional careers in diplomacy and other actions to anticipate and prevent wars and other violent conflict? Such a question is rarely asked, so is it surprising that we aren't given a chance to discuss the answers? Democracy includes knowing what questions are not asked that need to be asked. Such thoughts prompted Congressman Dennis Kucinich (Dem. Ohio) to introduce in 2001 a bill that would create a Department of Peace. Isn't that a worthy project for America's youngsters to adopt?

Waging Peace, Not War

Almost everyone, if given a choice, would like to live in peace instead of living in a war zone. You've probably seen many movies about war—explosions, people screaming and running, buildings on fire, bodies torn apart, medics trying to help, sirens, and so forth. Exciting, gripping. Have you seen movies about making peace and avoiding war? Too boring? What people fear or hate that ends in violence winds up in many profitable movies, cartoons, graphic novels, and books. What people like to grow up with—a peaceful home, neighborhood, community, and country—less often appears on the screen. When you go to your place of worship, you listen to sermons about peace. Major religions teach that peace is the way to go, not war, death, and destruction. Yet our federal government spends over half of its operating budget on war and preparing for war, and very little on waging peace to forestall or reduce the conflicts that lead to war. Don't you think something is out of balance here?

Many of our holidays speak of past wars and victories. There are military parades and battle hymns and martial music. Our national anthem, "The Star-Spangled Banner," came out of the War of 1812 against the British. The more history you study, the more you'll read about waging wars. But can't peace also be waged, thought about, and honored? This has worked well whenever tried, as with peace treaties or successful peace movements. Wars have taken hundreds of millions of lives—women, children, men—and wounded far larger numbers. Wars destroy schools, homes, and hospitals and poison the environment—the air, the water, the land. Wars take huge sums of money away from what people need to live good lives. Wars usually end up taking away some of our freedoms even after the wars end. (For a good example, look up the Patriot Act.) If we spend so much time on wars, something we don't like, why do we spend so little time on peace and nonviolence, which we do like? We all need to ponder these questions deeply and discuss them with family and friends.

Colman McCarthy and Peace Studies

You've already met Colman McCarthy briefly. Well educated, happily married with three grown sons, he was a prominent columnist for the *Washington Post* for many years. He biked to work, played golf and wrote a lot about it, produced articles and books, and for nearly three decades lived a good comfortable life as a vegan, an avid cyclist, and an animal rights advocate. Earlier in his life as a reporter, he decided to become a *peace correspondent*, figuring there were plenty of war correspondents. He covered the activities of Martin Luther King Jr. in the late 1960s and traveled to interview famous people who "were offering solutions to the world's violence." Colman wrote about his interviews with Mother

Teresa, Archbishop Desmond Tutu, Ireland's Mairead Corrigan and Seán MacBride, Argentina's Adolfo Pérez Esquivel, and Muhammad Yunus of Bangladesh, all Nobel Prize winners. He'd always ask them how to go about increasing peace and decreasing violence, and they would say, "Go where the people are." To Colman that meant the schools.

One day, a poor public school in Washington, DC, invited him to teach a course on creative writing. Colman replied, "I'd rather teach peace." And off he went, starting peace courses at high schools and colleges and law schools in the DC area. Then he went all around the country urging teachers and principals and deans to start peace studies at their high schools and colleges. In 1970, only one college had a peace studies course. By 2011, there were more than five hundred. Colman and his wife, Mavourneen, founded the Center for Teaching Peace in 1985, which led to his greatest book, *I'd Rather Teach Peace*. You can't imagine how well he holds the attention of middle school and high school students until you see him in action. He doesn't believe in grades. He tells students, "Instead of asking questions, be bolder and question the answers. The most important 'answer' to question is the idea that violence leads to peace. If violence were truly effective, we would have had peace eons ago." He gives the examples of India and South Africa, which could have had the bloodiest of wars for independence if not for the great peace leaders Mahatma Gandhi, who perfected nonviolent civil disobedience, and Nelson Mandela, who, after being released from twenty-eight years in prison under a racist apartheid regime, chose reconciliation as his pathway to the victory of peace. Colman has many examples of brutal governments that were overthrown by people "who had no army, no bombs, and no bullets," as in the Philippines, in Chile, in Poland, in Yugoslavia and Georgia and Czechoslovakia, for instance. His students learn about the lives of these and many other peacemakers for the first time by reading their writings. He wants the students to tell him what's on their minds, to challenge him, to come to the head of the class with him and talk about their reactions or doubts.

With thirty-six thousand high schools and about seventy-eight thousand elementary schools in our country, peace studies needs much broader acceptance. How about your schools?

One visit from Colman, and this mind-opening subject of such importance for your lives may become part of your classes. His first question is to ask his audience how many have ever taken a peace course. Very few hands go up. Whereupon Colman says, "If this were a peace-loving, peace-seeking and peace building-society, every hand would have gone up. We all graduate as peace illiterates." He likes to quote Maria Montessori, a pioneering children's educator (there are Montessori schools all over the world), who once said, "Establishing lasting peace is the work of education."

Had there been one million experienced American peace advocates in 2003, President George W. Bush would not have dared launch an undeclared illegal war of brutal destruction on Iraq, with the chaos and violence continuing to this day. Millions of people, including children, were killed, seriously injured, or sickened. And tens of thousands of US soldiers were killed, injured, or sickened in George Bush's war against a country that never threatened us. As I said, there were children who were your age when that war and the war in Afghanistan started, and some are now in danger's way as soldiers. Studying peace lets you anticipate the early signs leading to violent conflict and head it off. Most war historians know that. Most soldiers come back hating wars and the violence they generate long after they have ended.

Just listen to World War II five-star general Dwight D. Eisenhower, who was elected our president in 1952. On April 16, 1953, he addressed the American Society of Newspaper Editors with a speech titled "The Chance for Peace," sometimes known as "The Cross of Iron" speech. The spring of 1953, about eight years after World War II ended, was a time when fear and force again dominated world politics as two superpowers, the Soviet Union and the United States, faced off against each other. Here, in part, is what President Eisenhower said.

> **The worst to be feared and the best to be expected can be simply stated. The worst is atomic war. The best would be this: a life of perpetual fear and tension; a burden of arms draining the wealth and labor of all peoples; a wasting of strength that defies the American system, or the Soviet system, or any system to achieve true abundance and happiness for the peoples of this earth.**
>
> **Every gun that is made, every warship launched, every rocket fired signifies, in the final sense, a theft from those who hunger and are not fed, those who are cold and are not clothed.**

This world in arms is not spending money alone. It is spending the sweat of its laborers, the genius of its scientists, the hopes of its children. The cost of one modern heavy bomber is this: a modern brick school in more than 30 cities. It is two electric power plants, each serving a town of 60,000 population. It is two fine, fully equipped hospitals. It is some fifty miles of concrete highway. We pay for a single fighter plane with a half million bushels of wheat. We pay for a single destroyer with new homes that could have housed more than 8,000 people.

This is, I repeat, the best way of life to be found on the road the world has been taking. This is not a way of life at all, in any true sense. Under the cloud of threatening war, it is humanity hanging from a cross of iron. These plain and cruel truths define the peril and point the hope that come with this spring of 1953.

This is one of those times in the affairs of nations when the gravest choices must be made, if there is to be a turning toward a just and lasting peace. It is a moment that calls upon the governments of the world to speak their intentions with simplicity and with honesty. It calls upon them to answer the question that stirs the hearts of all sane men: Is there no other way the world may live?

No later president ever spoke such frank words or made such scathing comparisons between the cost of war and civilian needs at home. His successors all brought us, with varying degrees of militarism, into the arms race and the future which President Eisenhower dreaded.

History books describe military heroes but ignore the contributions of peacemakers who try to head off bloody conflicts. If you read about World War I and what event in Serbia ignited this totally avoidable war that killed over twenty million people, you'll see what I mean. And it's not just wars. As you know, there is violence in homes, on the streets, at schools, in the workplace, and more subtle violence stemming from many dangerous consumer products, such as unsafe cars and drugs, and from the pollution that surrounds many of us in the environment and workplace. In the words of Ian Harris, the author of *Peace Education*, peace studies "question the structures of violence that dominate every day." In your own daily experience, you shouldn't have much trouble concentrating your mind on such harms. You can learn how to shape the future for peace. How can you not? As the aforementioned Howard Zinn wrote, "History is full of instances of successful resistance—although we are not informed very much about this—without violence and against tyranny, by people using strikes, boycotts, and a dozen ingenious forms of struggle."

Everywhere he goes, Colman McCarthy says, "Marches are fine, protests are fine, but it's in schools where things really happen." He has changed many a life by exploring the power of peace with his students. He describes some of these students and what they became in his book *I'd Rather Teach Peace*.

Animal Welfare and Respecting Nature

Decades ago, few questions were asked about the well-being of the animal kingdom or about the frequently expressed boast that mankind must have dominion over nature. Before the environmental and animal rights movements got underway, we had simplistic ideas about our domesticated pets. Fido the dog was loyal, "man's best friend." We had little idea of the intelligence of dogs beyond what we could train them to do. We knew that they could probably hear, see, and smell much better than humans, but not to such an extent as later studies have shown. Cats were cuddly but could be temperamental. Cartoons gave us cute Mickey Mouse and silly Donald Duck. Entertaining jungle novels and movies like the *Tarzan of the Apes* gave us lasting, largely fictional images of lions, tigers, elephants, and other wild creatures.

Children of all cultures around the world love animals and often want them as pets. They know more about various kinds of animals from their televisions and their computers than my generation did. They are learning in some countries, including the US, that mistreating pets and wild animals such as squirrels can get them in trouble with the law. Increasingly, strong penalties are being enforced against torturing animals, even those raised to be slaughtered for their meat. There are more and more vegetarians who recoil over the cruelty of packed chicken, pig, and cattle pens. Psychologists have found that children who are cruel to animals are predisposed to becoming cruel or violent toward humans as adults. Everywhere, it seems, there are kind animal rescuers, people who adopt strays, people ready to report abuses to local animal control offices. Groups have been formed to save wolves, tigers, lions, elephants, rhinos, the American bison, dolphins, whales, condors, and other creatures from extinction, successfully turning the tide in some instances.

Other organized initiatives have slowed or stopped the use of chimps, rabbits, and beagles in scientific and commercial research because of the inhumane methods involved. For scientific purposes, new tests have been devised that don't use animals. Even the cosmetics companies are finally learning to abandon their utterly cruel treatment of beagles and rabbits.

All these trends, driven by citizen power, are heartening, but your generation needs to go deeper in your understanding and communion with the natural world. Coupled as you are with your cell phones and other electronic gadgetry, you're probably spending less time in nature than any children in human history. You may be participating in organized sports, but just playing outdoors with your friends is getting to be rarer and rarer. Not being outdoors regularly is not good for your health. The medical community calls this condition "nature insufficiency." You need what sunlight, air, water, gardening, hiking, and curiosity can do for your body and your mind. German educators who have begun to hold classes outdoors find that both they and their students benefit. The experience stimulates a variety of awarenesses and lessons that result when you immerse yourself in nature.

Here I want to tell you about a wonderful tradition. "One Child + One Bus Ticket = A World of Possibilities" is the compelling message of the Fresh Air Fund, established in 1877 to give New York City children from low-income families the opportunity to spend the summertime with host families or at a sleepaway camp in the countryside, the opportunity to experience putting their feet on soil for the first time before they go home to the city and its cement sidewalks and playgrounds. In the meantime, they've had a learning experience, often over consecutive years, that opens up a whole new world to them. Most important is the lesson that human beings are an intricate part of the natural world, interacting with all living species, including with each other, in a way that must include knowledge and understanding so we can act in an ecologically rational manner. I was raised in a rural area, and because of my parents' teachings, I learned to appreciate the bounty of our small landscape—the fruit trees in our yard, pears and apples, and also a concord grape arbor. Can you imagine that if you live in a city?

The Fresh Air Fund enables children to commune with nature and to learn by doing. For example, want to go fishing? First you have to dig for worms as bait for the fish, and then you will feel the inviting warmth of the soil and come to learn the immense value of worms in keeping the land fertile. Wouldn't you end the day more observant, self-confident, and ready for what comes next? Maybe you and your family have hosted a Fresh Air child. Maybe you've been one yourself. If so, you can testify firsthand to the joys and benefits of the program.

Let's go back to that old faithful, curiosity. What humans used to call "dumb animals" are really just the opposite. They have multiple intelligences for survival, adaptation, and procreation that are beyond astonishing. Just watch squirrels, surrounded by dangers and enemies, make it through the season, storing food, creating nests safe from hawks, doing high-wire leaps from twig to twig without falling to the ground, even figuring out which acorns can be saved for storage and which have to be eaten right away.

Consider the engineering skills of beavers building dams in their hydraulic environs in all kinds of weather. The sensitivity of octopi and their instant adaptabilities have stunned marine biologists who are amazed by this aquatic animal's intelligence. Bees, ants, spiders, and the critical earthworms beneath the soil have abilities that not only shame human capabilities but are teaching our species important scientific insights, not to mention adding their crucial value to the environment.

Indeed, the more we respect the intelligence of natural creatures from mammals down to birds, fishes, reptiles, and the fascinating world of insects, the more we discover the interconnected roles of biological systems, including our own. The more we respect the habitats of these animal species, the more we will take care of our own habitats. The reverse has been all too true for centuries. When we destroy animal habitats, we end up destroying human habitats. Consider the clear-cutting of forests, widespread soil erosion, and the decline of fisheries in polluted lakes and oceans. The first rule of ecology, wrote environmental scientist Barry Commoner, "is that everything is connected to everything else."

Our scientists are discovering the ways in which other species see, hear, smell, and maneuver better than we do. They are increasing their knowledge of zoonotic (animal-connected) diseases, such as AIDS, malaria, Ebola, and avian influenza. In 2020, we faced a new threat—the coronavirus, which causes Covid-19. We better become more humble, and stop to listen to the scientists. The "conquest of nature" is the arrogant path to our own omnicide. You are growing up at a time in human history when wonderful windows of discovery, systemic solution, and practical ecological sensitivity are opening wider and wider. The extinction of species used to be shrugged off, as with passenger pigeons, which went extinct over one hundred years ago when billions of them died through our hunting and deforestation of their habitats. Scientists now tell us that every species, no matter how "lowly," is a biological masterpiece that cannot be recovered once lost. Who knows what medicines, what technologies would have been derived from these lost species? We learned more about developing radar by observing the sonar capabilities of owls in the nighttime. The periwinkle plant in Madagascar produces chemicals that led to a cure for childhood leukemia. We are just at the very beginning of discoveries regarding this hugely varied biological and ecological wonder called Planet Earth. We should be alerted by a recent United Nations report on species extinction warning of its dire consequences for life on Earth.

If you choose, you can grow up being as environmentally unobservant as most of your elders were when they were children decades ago. Today you can lock yourself into cocoons of consumer gadgets and insulate yourself from the world of nature by spending your days inside looking at screens and text-messaging, which may titillate you but not teach you much. You may learn tactical skills that dig you deeper into your cocoon. Virtual reality goggles are heading for mass distribution, with the ensuing mass distraction, like few devices before. You can't ask yourself too early, "What is all this stuff doing to me?"

Let me make a suggestion. Pick yourself a giant evergreen tree with many branches stretching out on a nearly horizontal plane. This may be easier to do in the countryside, but cities have parks and arboretums. Sit a few yards away on the grass for several hours and start honing your observational skills, perhaps using binoculars. The solitude will be good for you, a healthful change of pace from your frenetic life. You'll see that this giant peaceful tree with its swaying branches has many visitors. Squirrels climb evergreens to escape a chasing cat, to chase each other and play, to build their nests, and who knows what else that sparks their imaginative ways of surviving day after day. Birds like evergreens for reasons that may not be immediately evident unless they're blatantly open about what they're doing, such as pecking for insects and other grub. After a while you can see even more as you refine your gaze. Maybe a book on evergreens will tell you more about the wildlife and insects that make their home or visit there, and then you'll have much more to watch for—spiders, beetles, lizards, maybe worms, butterflies, or caterpillars. The harder you look, the more you'll see in this mysterious world, one that the vast majority of humans never enter. To most it's just a tree from afar. To a landscape specialist, the tree shows more of itself and its health and its sturdiness. A botanist perceives more of the tree's complexity. The more intense your observation, the more your analytic talents will be enhanced. Your mind will find this progress enjoyable, just as people who go to art museums are more entranced the more they have trained themselves to perceive works of art by the masters. Teachers of writing may go a step further, asserting that your writing will improve as well.

Over fifty years ago, in 1968, Hart Day Leavitt published an amazing little book titled *The Writer's Eye*. Believing that creative perception is the key to vivid writing, he takes his readers into what he describes as "newer worlds of observation and thinking" by presenting many kinds of visual stimuli—photography, painting, advertisement, sculpture, diagram—in a hundred startling images produced by great artists in response to what they have experienced or imagined. Leavitt's aim is to help you sharpen your powers of artistic observation so that you can produce fresh and original writing. Keen observation, not test scores, is what improves your writing abilities. You might try keeping a journal, jotting down observations and ideas you want to develop. Becoming an effective writer early in life can take you a long way.

The Writer's Eye became a classic. It worked. Readers plunged into its world of artistry and emerged better writers. My nephew Tarek read it in the late seventies, when he was eleven, and saw his powers of observation sharpened. Not surprisingly, it was a factor in his becoming an excellent writer and editor. Other youngsters attest to the same experience. Their feedback reflects Leavitt's belief that "good writing is in a sense the result of observing with the eye and mind of an artist," of tapping into what he calls "the latent sense of artistry" in everybody.

At the end of his book, Leavitt leaves us with a passage of supreme wisdom. It is worth quoting in its entirety.

> **One of the greatest aims of education is to produce students who are able and willing to go on learning for the rest of their lives.**
>
> **Some people are born with this capacity, and they continue to extend themselves despite all obstacles. Others must first learn and then develop a technique that will sustain them into middle and old age; or else on the day they graduate they will stop dead, and never learn another new thing unless it makes money.**

Words worth reading more than once, in more time periods than one. Such observations reverberate throughout history. Consider the similar words of writer Samuel Smiles (1812-1904): "The spirit of self-help is the root of genuine growth in the individual."

A Fond Farewell

We have come to the end of our journey together, my young readers, about the importance and usefulness of self-education throughout your lifetime, with the aim of achieving a life well-lived. Again remember the words of Mark Twain, an avid practitioner of self-education who declared, "I have never let my schooling interfere with my education." Twain took every opportunity to expand his learning, working as a journeyman printer, a Mississippi steamboat pilot, and a Nevada miner before he started writing seriously.

Richard Feynman, Nobel Prize-winning physicist, was "an authentic intellectual who became a pop-culture hero," wrote Freeman Dyson, another renowned physicist. Feynman's honesty, his ability to make complex ideas understandable, and his ever-present humor shone through his writings and talks. In expressing his appreciation for the Nobel Prize, he informed the Swedish Academy that he already had the prize. "The prize is the pleasure of finding things out," he said.

As the drums leading to World War II in the 1930s got louder, one of our leading poets, Edna St. Vincent Millay, illuminated a major challenge of her time and also ours. In our day, as in hers, there is plenty of data from which we can fashion the knowledge we need to solve or diminish pressing societal problems, but Millay reminds us of a critical missing element that obstructs our search for solutions. She wrote memorably:

> Upon this gifted age, in its dark hour,
> Rains from the sky a meteoric shower
> Of facts . . . they lie unquestioned, uncombined.
> Wisdom enough to leech us of our ill
> Is daily spun; but there exists no loom
> To weave it into fabric . . .

As you move to create a fulfilling life, keep these inspiring words in the forefront of your mind. Keep your eyes on the loom.

One of the shortest and most thoughtful college graduation speeches I know of was given by Sam Maloof, a renowned and completely self-taught woodworker. He first delivered it in 2006 at the University of California, Riverside, and then in 2007 at California State University in San Bernardino and Mt. San Antonio College. I leave you to contemplate his helpful advice.

SAM MALOOF ON WORK AND LIFE

I was really very surprised when I was asked to address you today. I did not graduate from college.

I did not even attend college. There could only be two possible reasons I have been invited to speak to you—perhaps it is because I am known for designing and making chairs, or—perhaps it is because I am 91 years old and still working my trade and loving it.

What I should be known for is having chosen a life that has brought me success and happiness.

So, I will tell you what I know about how to make a chair.

First—the legs—the support for the chair. They are the foundation. They are what hold you up ... values, principles and beliefs—make sure you have enough legs.

The arms—something to hold on to. They are the friends, partners and family who embrace you ... choose them carefully.

The back—the back keeps you upright and steady—and helps you look straight ahead—to focus on your goals. The back should be strong and comfortable.

The seat—does it sit well? Specifically, does it fit you? Choose your heart's desire. Be sure it is your choice, your chosen path.

As you journey through life—reflect on what will be your legs—your arms—your back—your seat.

Good chairs are not made of straight lines but of many curves—and so will be your life.

So this is what I have learned about making a chair that can serve for a lifetime, something that you will enjoy sitting in—and others will also appreciate.

Now, because you are smart, young college graduates, you already know that when I say "This is how to build a chair," you know what I really mean is—"This is how you build your life."

You are the artist and designer—so go build your chair thoughtfully and construct a worthy and happy life.

I wish blessings and peace for each of you.

And so do I. Thank you for listening!

INDEX

abortion, 11
abstraction, 48-49
achievement, 59-60
activism, 2, 5-6, 25-29, 151-52, 193. *See also* citizen action
Adams, John, 105
Addams, Jane, 127
addictions, 74-75, 84-85, 97, 143
adults, 146
   need to encourage children, 1, 23
   failings of, 12, 23-24, 40-41, 150-51, 159, 169
   influence of children on, 7
advertising, 36-40
   misleading, 37, 155-56
   targeted at children, 12, 36-37, 77-78, 141-43, 154, 178
al-Ghazali, Abu Hamid, 169-70, 199
alcohol industry, 37, 39
Alhambra, Spain, 129-30
Amazon.com, Inc., 171
American Civil Liberties Union, 126-27
American Museum of Tort Law, 179-82, 202
American Psychological Association, 26
American Society of News Editors, 12, 211
Anderson, Jack, 8
Anderson, Ray C., 100-101
animals, 214-19
Apple Corporation, 78, 177
arbitration, 176
attention span, 55. *See also* concentration

Babe the Blue Ox (legend), 35-36
Baldwin, Roger N., 127
Barnard, Anne, 5
Bartlett's Familiar Quotations, 56-57
beauty. *See* cosmetics
Bell, Alexander Graham, 117, 124-25

Bell, Cavanaugh, 4, 7
Beyond Pesticides, 6
bicycles, 29-30
Bittman, Mark, 135
Blake, William, 22
body, functions of, 147-50
Body Shop International, Ltd., 164
Braille, 122
Brandeis, Louis D., 54
Bridges, Ruby, 45, 48
Brinkley, David, 11
Brown & Williamson Tobacco Corporation, 38
Brown v. Board of Education (1954), 43
bullying, 4-5, 97, 164, 183
Burger King, 39
Bush, George W., 8, 47, 204, 210-11
business. *See* corporate crime; corporate power; corporate welfare
Butler, Smedley D., 204

Califano, Joseph A., Jr., 41
Campaign for Tobacco-Free Kids, 188
Canada, 66
capitalism, 83

Carnegie, Andrew, 87
Carper, Jean, 142
Carr, Nicholas, 179
Carus, Marianne, 2
cash. *See* currency
cellular telephones. *See* mobile telephones
Center for Science in the Public Interest, 140
Centers for Disease Control, 145
charity, 4-5, 29-30, 86-87, 193-94
Chavez, Cesar, 203
Cheney, Dick, 204
child labor, 65, 111, 190
childhood, concept of, 46
Children's Express, 10-12, 163
Children's Online Privacy Protection Act of 1998, 177
chores, 62
Chouinard, Yvon, 101
Cicero, 53
cigarette smoking, 185-88. *See also* tobacco industry; vaping
citizen action, 186-95. *See also* activism
citizenship, 23
civil rights, 11, 43-45, 127
Civil War, 65, 110
Clampitt, Robert, 10-11
climate crisis. *See* global warming

coal industry, 8, 36, 65, 66, 154, 184
Coles, Robert, 43-46, 71
Columbus, Christopher, 63-64
Commoner, Barry, 217
computers, 13, 94, 139, 200
    advertisements on, 37, 77
    fallibility of, 50-51
    as information sources, 160, 214
    overuse of, 23, 75, 144
    remote learning and, 16
concentration, 22, 25, 28, 31. *See also* attention span
Confederate States of America, 65
consumer education, 21, 139-41, 156-57, 183-84
consumer protection, 11, 37-38, 98-99, 193, 213
Consumer Reports, 156
contracts, 17, 98, 167-70, 173-76, 179, 183
controlling processes, 78, 96-98
conversations, 1, 9, 88, 90-91, 133
coronavirus. *See* COVID-19
corporate crime, 8, 98, 99, 172
corporate power, 96-100, 170, 183-84
corporate welfare, 99-100
cosmetics, 163-67

Costa Rica, 152
COVID-19, 13, 16, 75, 156, 217
Crawford, Matthew B., 94
credit cards, 170-72
Cricket, 2
critical thinking, 84-85, 153
currency, 170-73
curiosity, 22, 34-35
    of animals, 216-17
    exercising of, 31-32
    of Benjamin Franklin, 103, 105
    of Helen Keller, 117
    social action and, 24-25, 28, 42
    a valuable attribute, 84

Davis, Daryl, 24
Debs, Eugene, 126
deceptions, 36-40, 143, 164-67, 174-78
deforestation, 35-36, 65
democracy, 54, 65, 180, 185, 189, 206
Dewey, John, 69, 107, 201
Dickinson, Emily, 198
dictionary, 49-57
discipline, 61-62, 73, 107, 150, 195-98
disease, 38-42

business and, 98
lack of exercise and, 161-62
junk food and, 39-40, 145-46
tobacco, vaping, alcohol and, 38-39, 41-42, 85, 96-97, 143, 148
zoonotic, 217-18
dissent, 153
distractions, 57, 125, 130, 195, 219. *See also* screens and screentime
District of Columbia Water Department, 94-96
Donahue, Phil, 140
Douglas, Mike, 140
Douglass, Frederick, 109-16, 127-28, 198, 201-2
Doukas, Dimitra, 192
Duncan, Winston, 29-30

Earth Day, 5
Eastman, Crystal, 127
Einstein, Albert, 22, 58
Eisenhower, Dwight D., 211-13
Elizabeth II (queen), 165
empathy, 85-86
environment. *See* deforestation; global warming; pollution
expectation levels, 7, 15-16, 61

Facebook (corporation), 81, 99, 168, 171, 174-75, 178
facts, 154-57
family, 31, 60, 77-79, 87-93
Federal Communications Commission, 79, 187
Federal Trade Commission, 38, 94, 177
FedEx Corporation, 171
Feldman, Jay, 6
Fellmeth, Robert C., 174
Feynman, Richard P., 222
Financial Crisis of 2008, 99
Finkbeiner, Felix, 2-3, 7, 195
Flint, Mich., 97
Fonda, Jane, 151
Food and Drug Administration, 166-67
Ford, Gerald R., 11
Founding Fathers, 65-66, 105, 179
frames of reference, 20-21, 127-33
Franklin, Benjamin, 61, 102-9, 110, 127-28, 142, 201
free things, 17-18
freedom, 53-54
Fresh Air Fund, 215-16
friendship, 18
Fromm, Erich, 53

Gaiman, Neil, 51
Gandhi, Mahatma, 91-92, 209
Gardner, Howard E., 60
Gardner, John W., 70
Garrison, William Lloyd, 112
General Accounting Office, 167
General Motors, 38
George III (king), 202
Gilbert High School (Winsted, Conn.), 34, 191
Giles, Gilbert, 10
global warming, 67, 155
    protests and, 2, 24-27, 31, 72, 151
    renewable fuels and, 23, 151
    trees and, 3
"good ancestors," 10-12, 150-52
Google, Inc., 168, 171, 177
gratitude, 18-19
Griffin, Merv, 140
grown-ups. *See* adults

Halpern, Jake, 32
Hammacher Schlemmer & Co., 156
Harris, Ian M., 213
Harty, Sheila, 154
Hawken, Paul G., 146-47, 151
health, 133-42, 161-63
helpfulness, 18

Herbert, Martha, 70-71
Hoffmann, Banesh, 58
holidays, 202-4, 207
Holmes, Oliver Wendell, 90
Hume, Brit, 8
Huxley, Aldous, 154-55, 201

idealism, 60
    of children, 1-2, 6-10, 14, 47-48
    self-censorship and, 30-32
    social action and, 24-27, 151-52, 195
imagination, 31-32, 85
    of children, 1-2, 22-24, 28
    exercising of, 218-21
    Helen Keller and, 124
Industrial Workers of the World, 126
inequality, 14, 66
infant formula, 40, 78
infant mortality, 66
Instagram (application), 81
intellect, 57, 85, 128, 198. *See also* intelligence
intelligence, 57, 60, 72. *See also* intellect; testing
Interface Corporation, 100-101
internet, 16-17, 176-79
inventors, 23, 80-81, 105, 117

Iraq War, 47, 151, 204-6, 210
Iroquois, 64

Jacobson, Michael F., 37-38, 140-41
Jacoby, Russell, 84
Jefferson, Thomas, 14, 105, 154
Johnson, James Weldon, 127
Johnson, Lyndon B., 41, 127
Johnson, Nicholas, 79
junk food, 12. *See also* nutrition; obesity
    advertisements for, 36-37, 96, 156
    campaigns against, 139-41
    disease and, 84, 134-35, 147
    obesity and, 39-40, 135
justice, 54-55, 60, 198
JUUL Labs, Inc., 143

Kallos, Ben J., 5-6
Keller, Helen, 116-28
Kidron (baroness), 178
King, Martin Luther, Jr., 24, 208
King, Stephen, 51
Kraft, Robert K., 100
Kucinich, Dennis, 206-7

LaDuke, Winona, 151
LaVoie, Charlene, 191
leaf blowers, 76
"learning by doing," 69-71
Leavitt, Hart Day, 220-21
Lewis, Barbara A., 28
Library of Congress, 88
Liliuokalani (queen), 128-29
Lincoln, Abraham, 54
Lorillard Tobacco Company, 38
love, 18, 45, 121-22

Maathai, Wangari, 2-3
Madison, James, 105
make-up. *See* cosmetics
Maloof, Sam, 223-24
Mandela, Nelson, 209-10
manual arts, 93-94
manual labor, 68
Margolin, Jamie, 26
Marjory Stoneman Douglas High School (Parkland, Fla.), 26, 152
marketing. *See* advertising
maturity, 11, 43-49, 88, 109, 133
Mayo Clinic, 145
Mazur, Laurie Ann, 37
McCarthy, Colman, 34, 208-13
McDonald's Corporation, 39, 78, 141, 147

McKibben, Bill, 151
medical malpractice, 182
medieval society, 46, 178
Messud, Claire, 165
Mexican War, 64
Middle Ages. *See* medieval society
Millay, Edna St. Vincent, 222-23
Milleron, Tarek, 220
mind, 19-21, 33-34, 43, 50, 71, 84-86, 108, 133, 139, 146, 196-97, 215
mobile telephones
 advertisements on, 37, 77
 contracts and, 168, 173
 overuse of, 22, 75, 91, 144
 remote learning with, 16
 shredding of English language and, 51
 sleep deprivation and, 177
 unhealthy attachment to, 31, 178, 215
Mondale, Walter F., 10
Monteiro, Carlos A., 135
Montessori, Maria, 210
Morley, John (viscount), 57
Murrow, Edward R., 185
myths, 35-36, 63-67

Nader, Laura, 97-98, 153

Nader, Nathra, 19, 67-68, 86, 195, 199
Nader, Ralph, 7-8, 53, 66, 88-89, 135-36, 158
Nader, Rose, 32, 135-36, 138-39, 166, 193-94, 199
Nader, Shafeek, 49-50, 62, 64, 94, 128-29, 191-92
Nancy Drew (character), 40
National Center on Addiction and Substance Abuse, 41
National Public Radio, 12, 88
nature, importance of, 214-21
Nestle S.A., 78
Newman, Richard L., 180-81
news media, 8, 48, 194-95, 205
 children and, 10-12, 27-29
 exposés by, 166
 tobacco industry and, 188
Newton, Isaac, 22
Nobel Peace Prize, 3, 209
Northwestern Connecticut Community College, 192
nutrition, 133-42. *See also* junk food

Obama, Barack H., 47
obesity, 37, 39-40, 135, 161. *See also* junk food
organic food, 137-38

over-scheduled, 61-62. *See also* solitude
Owen, Penny, 72-74, 89
ownership, 76-78, 82-83
Oxford English Dictionary, 50, 153-54

Page, Joseph A., 182
Paine, Thomas, 205
Palestinians, 8
Panchyk, Richard, 184
pandemic. *See* COVID-19
parents, undermined by corporations, 136-37
Patagonia, Inc., 101
Patriotic Millionaires, 87
patriotism, 19, 152-53
Patton, George S., 205
Paul Bunyan (legend), 35-36
peace, 34, 203, 206-13
peer groups, 30-33, 46-47, 84, 107
Pelletier, Autumn, 3-4, 7
penmanship, 51-52
Pertschuk, Michael, 187
pesticides, 5-6, 97
Pfizer, Inc., 38
pharmaceutical industry, 36-38, 82-83, 166
Philip Morris International, Inc., 38, 186

Phillips, Wendell, 111
physical education, 161-63
Pine Ridge Indian Reservation, 4
Plautus, 56
pollution, 1, 7, 65, 183, 213
    caused by business, 34, 97-98
    Ronald Reagan on, 9
    Superfund and, 27
postal service, 61, 77, 104, 203
poverty, 1, 14, 28, 66, 70, 152
printing press, 199
privacy, 17, 98-99, 171, 173-74, 176-79, 191
progress, 185-95
Project Citizen, 28-29, 35
propaganda, 153-57
proverbs, 199-202
psychological disorders, 70-71
public airwaves, 12, 79-82
Public Citizen, 145
public service, 70
"pursuit of happiness," 13-14, 108

questioning authority, 6-9, 45, 187, 209
Quintilian, 56

R. J. Reynolds Tobacco
    Company, 186
Rabi, I. I., 34
racism, 23-24, 43-45, 110-15,
    184
Radin, Margaret, 176
Rankin, Jeannette, 127
Rao, Gitanjali, 80
Reagan, Ronald, 9
Reed, Ken, 161-63
regulation, 98-99
reverie, 62
Revolutionary War, 106, 183,
    205
Reynolds, Janet, 191
rhetoric, 51
Rockefeller, Nelson A., 11
Rockwell, Norman, 45
Roddick, Anita, 164-66
Rogovin, Paula, 6, 7
Rowland, John G., 100
Rowling, J. K., 51

Safe Drinking Water Act of
    1974, 95
Sanders, Bernard, 87
Scholastic, 158
Schultz, Brian, 29, 35, 185
science-based arguments, 2, 25,
    38, 137, 155, 218

screens and screentime, 13, 16,
    177-79
  as distraction, 57
  excessive use of, 23, 51, 55, 75,
    144
seat belts, 7, 42
self-censorship, 30-31, 153
self-consciousness, 6-7
self-discipline, 61-62, 73, 107
self-education, 61-63, 68, 71-74,
    102-29, 195-96
self-reliance, 7, 17, 71, 107, 123-
    24, 139, 195
Seventeen, 46-47
Shafeek Nader Trust for the
    Community Interest, 74
Shakespeare, William, 197
Singletary, Michelle, 170
skilled trades, 68, 193. *See also*
    manual arts
Slack, Warner V., 59
slavery, 63, 65, 110-14, 184
Small Business Administration,
    86
smart, 57-61. *See also* intelligent
smartphone. *See* mobile
    telephone
Smiles, Samuel, 221
social action. *See* citizen action
social injustice, 6-7, 70, 124, 184
social media, 4, 36, 81
Social Venture Network, 101

Index   233

socialism, 126
Socrates, 76
soda pop, 12, 135, 137. *See also* junk food
Sokolowski, Peter, 54-55
solar energy, 67
solitude, 61-63, 198, 219-20
spoiled children, 46
Stein, Gertrude, 34-35
StoryCorps, 88
Strunk, William, Jr., 197-98
sugar, 134-35, 137. *See also* junk food
Sullivan, Anne, 117, 120-24
Superfund, 27

taboos, 183-85, 188
tattoos, 32-33
taxes
  on cigarettes, 187
  funding corporate welfare, 99-100
  funding public services, 90-91, 194
  funding science and technology, 67, 82
  funding wars, 47-48
  on wealth, 86-87
technology, 15, 56-57, 67, 179, 185, 218. *See also* computers;

mobile telephones
teenagers, 1, 32-33, 46, 96, 130, 163, 188
television programming, 80-82
Tennyson, Alfred (lord), 56
Terry, Luther L., 38, 186
tests, 13, 15, 57-59, 153
"This Land Is Your Land," 6
Thomas, Helen, 8
Thunberg, Greta, 2, 7, 15, 24-27, 31, 71-72, 151, 195
time, 88-89, 92
tobacco industry, 36-38, 41, 96-97, 142-43, 185-88
tort law, 179-83
traits, 1, 18-19, 22, 59-60
Trudeau, Justin P. J., 3
Trump, Donald J., 72
truth, 153-57
Twain, Mark, 13, 221-22

United Nations, 2-4, 25, 27, 218
United States Constitution, 54, 104, 106, 110, 127, 175, 179, 205
United States Department of Agriculture, 137-38, 142
United States Forest Service, 36
unlearn, 13, 62-63, 67-68

vaping, 143, 188
vegetarianism, 25, 141
violence, 1. *See also* war
   committed by adults, 23, 47-48, 151
   committed by businesses, 98, 213
   in neighborhoods, 14, 70, 213
   in schools, 10-11, 26, 43-45, 213
   as self-destructive personal behavior, 84
   in video games, 75
voting, 157-60

wisdom, 56, 196
Wolz, Alex, 30
women's suffrage, 110, 116, 184
World Health Organization, 40
World War I, 213
World War II, 154, 205, 211, 222
writing, 197-98, 220-21

Zero Hour, 26
Zinn, Howard, 206, 213

Wang, Yangming, 134
war, 204-8, 210-11
warning labels, 38-39, 143
Warren, Elizabeth, 87
water, 3-4, 80-81, 94-96, 190
Webster's Dictionary, 52, 54-55
Wells Fargo & Company, 172
"what if?," 23-24
White, E. B., 197-98
Whitehead, Alfred North, 83, 118, 195-97
"why" questions, 1, 6-8, 11
Winchester, Simon, 83
Winsted, Conn., 190-94
Winterson, Jeanette, 50

ABOUT THE AUTHOR

Claire Nader is a political scientist and author recognized for her work on the impact of science on society. She is an advocate for numerous causes at the local, national and international level. As the first social scientist working at the Oak Ridge National Laboratory, she joined pioneering initiatives in energy conservation and the multifaceted connections between science, technology and public policy. While at Oak Ridge she organized a groundbreaking global conference (1967) on Science and Technology in Developing Countries and co-edited the conference proceedings with Professor A.B. Zahlan (Cambridge University Press, 1969).

Later she worked to improve corporate and governmental policies affecting communities through a variety of projects and nonprofit institutions. For ten years she chaired the Council for Responsible Genetics in Cambridge, MA. She founded the Winsted Health Center Foundation advocating for locally controlled health care. And for thirty-two years she has administered the Joe A. Callaway Award for Civic Courage in Washington, D.C.